The Hungry
Archaeologist
in France

The River Dordogne at La Roque Gageac

THE HUNGRY
ARCHAEOLOGIST
IN FRANCE

A Travelling Guide
to
Caves, Graves and Good Living
in
the Dordogne and Brittany

by

GLYN DANIEL

FABER AND FABER
24 Russell Square
London

First published in mcmlxiii
by Faber and Faber Limited
24 Russell Square London WC1
Printed in Great Britain
by The Bowering Press Plymouth
All rights reserved

© *Glyn Daniel 1963*

Contents

Illustrations

PLATES

9

ILLUSTRATIONS

ILLUSTRATIONS

TEXT FIGURES

ILLUSTRATIONS

MAPS

DRAWINGS BY VILLIERS DAVID

Preface

Every year, and particularly in the late spring when people are beginning to plan their summer holidays, and again in June when archaeologically-minded undergraduates are working out their hitch-hikes across Europe, I get letters and requests for information about the prehistoric sites in France. Where are the most interesting and most accessible? How can one get to them? And how and where can one enjoy modestly the pleasures of French food and wine at the same time? It seemed to me, ten years ago, that it would be a saving of my own time as well as a better way of answering these requests, to put together some travel notes into a small book. This I did, and the small book was published under the title of *Lascaux and Carnac* by the Lutterworth Press in 1955. It seemed to have achieved its purpose which was to get people to some of the caves and graves of France, and to suggest hotels and cafés where they might prepare themselves for and restore themselves after their arduous archaeology. It is now out of print and, were it not so, needs revision since many of the details of prices, times and places have changed in the last decade.

This book is then a revision and expansion of *Lascaux and Carnac* and my hope is that it will prove as useful as in its first format. The travel information I have given should apply to the present; I checked it in the Dordogne last September and in Brittany last Christmas. This is a gossiping guide to some caves and graves in France. I have dealt mainly with only the two most famous areas in France—the Dordogne and the Morbihan, though Chapters VII, XI and XII give some account of sites outside these areas. Throughout I have dealt with all the areas described from the point of view of a most elementary introduc-

13

tion. This book is not a formal guide to the megaliths at Carnac or the Palaeolithic caves of the Dordogne. These are some of the things I would say if I met the reader at a café table at Carnac or on a hotel terrace in Montignac or Les Eyzies.

But then because we would have a glass of Muscadet or Monbazillac between us it would be so much nicer than a contact through the cold print of these pages. Since however that is how we would have met, I have given what help I can and my personal views on cafés and hotels. Only the most arid archaeology flourishes in France (or elsewhere) without good food and wine. I see that in *Lascaux and Carnac* I referred to the book as a mild essay in gastro-archaeology and that I used this neologism three times. That was a youthful indiscretion which now in the full pomposity of middle age I can happily repudiate. But I have been encouraged by my publisher to expand these aspects of the book and have done so.

It is now twenty years since I first visited Les Eyzies and thirty since I first went to Carnac. Since those first exciting visits I have spent a lot of time in both areas. Before the war I travelled often alone but sometimes with archaeological colleagues, and I well remember my early journeys in Brittany with J. M. de Navarro and T. G. E. Powell. Since the war my wife and I have travelled in Brittany and the Dordogne every year together and with many friends—Suzanne de St-Mathurin, Dorothy Garrod, Pierre-Roland Giot, Stuart Piggott, Paul Johnstone, the late Noël Small and Villiers David, to mention only a few. I am very happy to be able to include a few of Mr David's drawings made in Brittany in 1958. These brief chapters owe much to those in whose company I have come to know the Morbihan and the Dordogne, and most of all to my wife, whose maps have made the geography of these areas so clear.

Since 1954 two books have been published which are essential to the theme of this book. The first is *Brittany* by P-R. Giot in the *Ancient Peoples and Places* series (London, 1960) and the second is *The Caves of France and Northern Spain* by Ann and Gale Sieveking (London, 1962). The traveller using my book in the Dordogne should take with him also the Sievekings' book, and when he gets to Brittany should read Giot's book. The hungry traveller will not get much out of these books—it was not their purpose that he should—but they are indispensable to the archaeologist.

GLYN DANIEL

Les Eyzies—La Trinité—Cambridge
September 1962–January 1963

Acknowledgments

The sources of the illustrations are as follows: *Archives Photographiques* (Paris), Plates 5, 6, 7, 8, 9 (*a*), 11, 16 (*b*), 17 (*a*), 21, 22, 23 (*b*), and Figs. 5–8; Dr O. G. S. Crawford, Plates 18 (*a*), 25 (*b*); *Editions C.I.M.* (Mâcon), Plate 25 (*a*); Mrs Ruth Daniel, Plate 23 (*a*); Ray Delvert (Villeneuve-sur-Lot), Plate 3 (*b*); French Government Tourist Office, Plates 1, 13, 14, 15 (*a*), 18 (*b*); *Editions Gaby* (Arthaud, Nantes), Plates 20 (*b*), 24; Studio Guy-Rivière (Sarlat), Plate 2; *Editions Jos-le-Doaré* (Chateaulin), Plates 15 (*b*), 20 (*a*); Laborie (Bergerac), Plate 9; Lapie (Photothèque Française), Frontispiece, Plates 4, 16 (*a*); Mr Malcolm Murray (Department of Archaeology, Edinburgh), Plate 17 (*b*); Musée Miln-Le Rouzic (Carnac), Plate 19; Bernard Pierret, Plate 10 (*a*); *Editions Plassard* (Rouffignac) (Photo. René, Razac-sur-L'Isle), Plate 10 (*b*); Yan (J. Dieuzade, Toulouse), Plate 12; *Editions Yvon* (Paris), Plate 3 (*a*).

✠ I ✠

Introduction

There are many reasons for going to France, and they have often been rehearsed. The first is that it is the nearest foreign country to England and Wales, although perhaps Ireland and Belgium would dispute this claim. In twenty to twenty-five minutes' flying time you can nowadays be in France. With your bicycle, your scooter, your motor-cycle, or your car—or just yourself and your rucksack—you can report at Lydd, Southend or Hurn; the Customs and passport facilities are short; within a quarter of an hour of arriving you are in the air with the English Channel shining blue and gold below you. The Channel steamers are speeding across from Dover and Folkestone, but you get there ahead of them. The Customs and passport facilities on the French side are even shorter, because the French understand better than we do the importance of *le tourisme* to national economy, and in under half an hour from tightening your seat belt in Kent or Essex you are sitting down to your first *apéritif* on a café terrace. What is it to be, as the sun pours down on you, and, according as to whether you love or respect the sun, you position yourself under the gaily-striped umbrella? What is it to be? Dubonnet? Martini? Cinzano? St-Raphael? Which of these many names that have been pushed into your consciousness by the advertisements on the houses as you drove from the airport? Anyway, whichever it is, you are in France.

You are in another world. That is the second reason for France. It provides you with an entirely new way of life to sample and savour—a way of life with different drinking hours and eating habits and values. The essence of a holiday, we are told, is complete change. Crossing the English Channel provides that change, but it is not too violent a change. It is not the sort of violent change one is subjected to in flying to New Delhi or Cairo or Libreville, or even, for that matter, to south Spain or Malta. France provides a change within the framework of known experience and habits; it rings the changes on the customary pattern of known, experienced, enjoyed life in northwestern Europe. One does not feel, as one goes to France, that one has been very adventuresome, or that the natives are hostile.

There are two great reasons for visiting France—or so it seems to me, a professional archaeologist whose profession has so far still failed to dull his excitement in the material remains of the distant human past that happily survive to us, and whose eager appreciation of these archaeological remains is best sustained with a glass of the *vin de pays*. Of these two overwhelming reasons for visiting France, rather than Italy or Spain or Switzerland or the Low Countries, the first is its archaeological monuments, and the second its high traditions of eating and drinking—in a word, the living past and the eating present. And by its archaeological monuments I mean everything from Le Corbusier's *Cité* at Marseilles right back through time to the châteaux of the Loire and the Dordogne, the incomparable cathedrals, like Chartres and Bourges, the monuments of a time when France was part of the Roman Empire—the arch at Orange, the aqueduct at Pont du Gard, the theatres at Nîmes and Arles. What a magnificent feeling of the historical continuity and the antiquity of French civilization one gets when seeing some modern spectacle like a bullfight or a symphony concert in the *arènes* of Nîmes or Arles!

But Rome is less than a halfway house in the French past between Le Corbusier and the time, somewhere between 4500 and 4000 B.C., when the first peasant villagers came to France and introduced the crafts of pottery, domesticated animals and the cultivation of grain. As we British travel across and around France, it is the basic overwhelming agricultural tradition that impresses us; the peasant and the farmer are the backbone of French economy. This vital element in the structure of France did not exist before 4500 B.C. Before then, in France, as in Spain and in the British Isles, agriculture did not exist, and the way of life was by collecting fruits and berries and roots, by hunting animals and by fishing. The arrival of the first peasant farmers is thus, in some ways, the real beginning of French history. These first peasant farmers are the people whom archaeologists classify as Neolithic. As a professional archaeologist, it is the monuments of these first peasant farmers that interest me most in France, and particularly the tombs which some of these early farmers built in certain parts of France—the tombs which are referred to as megaliths.

Most people will have seen at some time or other a megalithic monument, or at least a photograph of one. Stonehenge is a megalithic monument, Avebury is another, and so are New Grange in Ireland, Bryn Celli Ddu in Wales and Stoney Littleton in Somerset. The word 'megalith' comes from two Greek words, *megas*, meaning large, and *lithos*, a stone, and all the five monuments I have mentioned, while varying very considerably among themselves, have this much in common: that they are built of very large stones. There are thousands of these megalithic monuments in western Europe—perhaps as many as 20,000, and France is particularly rich in them. No complete modern survey has been made of the megalithic monuments of France, but there probably exist at the present day at least 6,000 of them. Here lies one of the particular reasons why France interests me, as it does so many archaeologists—professional and amateur—who visit it: the magnificent archaeological megalithic monuments—splendid survivals of the beliefs and customs about death and religion of the inhabitants of western Europe in the third millennium B.C.

To someone with no knowledge of prehistoric archaeology it might seem that when you probe further back in human history than the time of the first peasant farmers, that is to say before 4500 to 4000 B.C. in western Europe, there remains little interesting or exciting to find. We are now back in pre-Neo-

lithic times, back among the food-gathering savages of the Old
Stone Age, or the Palaeolithic and Mesolithic of archaeological nomeclature. This Old Stone Age stretches back from
4500 B.C. to a date when man, in the sense of a tool-making
animal, came into existence and this date has been variously
estimated as three-quarters of a million to a million and a
quarter years ago. We have been going backward in our account
of the remote French past; let us reverse the process and go
forward, remembering some crucial dates. The first crude
human tools were being made in France between 600,000 and
1,000,000 years ago, the first agriculturists were living in France
at somewhere between 4500 and 4000 B.C. Known historical
civilization attested by literary records arrived in France round
about 600 B.C., when Greek Colonists from Phocaea settled at
Massilia—the present Marseilles. By 500 B.C. the Massiliotes
were penetrating Gaul by the Rhône-Saône valley, and by
300 B.C. their trade was spreading into the Rhine, and to the
Atlantic by the cross-country routes to Bordeaux and Nantes.
The Roman conquest of Gaul was effected by 52 B.C., and drew
the thin line of formal history across the page of the French past.

The uninformed traveller in France might well ask, is there
anything to interest me in that incredibly long period from the
beginning of human time to the arrival of the peasant farmers,
from 600,000 B.C. to 4000 B.C., and may be pardoned for sup-
posing that the answer would be a very firm negative. But it is
not so. The pre-Neolithic Stone Age used to be divided into
the Palaeolithic or Old Stone Age and the Mesolithic or Middle
Stone Age, and the Palaeolithic itself was divided into a Lower,
Middle and Upper. There has been a suggestion by two of the
most distinguished French prehistoric archaeologists, the late
Abbé Breuil and Professor Raymond Lantier, until recently
Director of the National Museum of Antiquities at St-Germain,
that the Upper Palaeolithic, which is in so many ways separate
from the Lower and Middle, should be called the Leptolithic,
but this suggestion has not as yet been widely adopted.[1] The

[1] H. Breuil and R. Lantier, *Les Hommes de la Pierre Ancienne* (Paris, 1951).
For other introductions to the Palaeolithic, see M. C. Burkitt, *The Old Stone*

suggestion merely emphasizes the fact that the Upper Palaeolithic (or Leptolithic) is a very separate phase of early human
history. During this phase the food-gathering savages created
a remarkable art, an art which, as we shall see, is almost certainly magico-religious in its origins and purpose. This is the
first art, or, to be more exact, the first surviving art of mankind,
and it occurs on ordinary objects of daily use—tools and
weapons—but also on the walls of rock shelters and caves. This
Upper Palaeolithic (or Leptolithic) art flourished somewhere
between 40,000 and 10,000 years ago, and is to be found mainly
in southern France and in Spain (particularly in the Cantabrian
Mountains). This is why it is often referred to as Franco-
Cantabrian art (Fig. 1).

Here, then, are the two main archaeological reasons why I go
to France and urge others to do the same; first, the great megalithic monuments of the third millennium B.C. and, second, the
painted and engraved caves; the earliest architecture and the
earliest art in north-western Europe. And there are two locali-
ties in France where these important and ancient aspects of
European culture may best be studied. The first is the neighbourhood of Carnac, a little town almost on the coast of south
Brittany and not far east of the Quiberon Peninsula; here there
is one of the most splendid and representative collections of
megalithic monuments in France, or in Europe, or in the world
—so much so that when to some people the word Carnac is
mentioned it means megaliths (and, by the way, there should
be no confusion with Karnak in Egypt; the names are quite
unconnected, though the two sites are archaeologically important). The second locality is the valleys of the Dordogne and
Vézère in southern France, particularly in the neighbourhood
of the little village of Les Eyzies and the little town of Montignac
or, as it has been calling itself since 1940, Montignac-Lascaux.

Age (1955); R. Lantier, *La Vie Préhistorique* (Paris, 1952); A. H. Brodrick,
Early Man (1948); A. Coates, *Prelude to History* (1951); L. S. B. Leakey,
Adam's Ancestors (1954); D. de Sonneville-Bordes, *L'Age de la Pierre* (in the
Que Sais-je series) (1961); and Jean Piveteau, *L'Origine de l'Homme: l'homme
et son passé* (1962).

Early Iron Age	750 B.C. to the Roman Conquest		
Bronze Age	1900 B.C.		
Chalcolithic	2500 B.C.		
Neolithic	4000 B.C.		
Mesolithic	10,000 B.C.		
Palaeolithic or Old Stone Age	Upper		
	Middle		
	Lower		

Fig. 1.   *The various periods into which French prehistory is divided, with approximate dates*

Here, in the beautiful Dordogne countryside, within a few miles of Les Eyzies and Montignac, are some of the most famous of the Upper Palaeolithic painted and engraved caves—Font de Gaume, Les Combarelles, La Mouthe, and, most famous of all since its accidental discovery in 1940, Lascaux. Here, then, are two main archaeological reasons for travel to France—the megaliths of Carnac and the Palaeolithic art of Lascaux and Les Eyzies. I do not know of two more exciting or agreeable possibilities for a holiday in France—possibilities which are so rewarding in their archaeology as well as in the charm of the countryside and the delights of good living.

I shall never forget my first visit to Carnac, nearly thirty years ago. I got off a main-line train from Brest to Paris and took the little departmental railway to Carnac—and who will not join with me in shedding a passing tear at the end of the French departmental railways, those exciting, dangerous, narrow-gauge railways that shrieked their brave way along the grass verges of the main roads, and, unprotected by gates, across these main roads and through woods and fields. They have been replaced by efficient buses, and I dare say it is no less exciting for the student-traveller to arrive at Carnac today in one of these buses from Vannes or Auray, the roof piled high with luggage and bicycles. But nothing will take away from me the memory of my arrival by departmental railway; I was an undergraduate with no spare cash and dragged my suitcase from the train up to the hotel above Carnac on the flanks of the Tumulus de St-Michel. It was a bright, hot, sunny June afternoon; in front of me a mile and a half away through the sand dunes and pine trees was the sea of the Bay of Quiberon. Behind me the countryside was studded with stone rows and great stone-chambered barrows—what subsequent history had left of the religion and hopes of the people who lived in France 4,000 to 5,000 years before. And I remember after dinner walking down to the great Carnac alignments and in the moonlight wandering along those miles of serried, large stones, their dark shadows a reminder of their darker past and our ignorance of their makers and builders. For me that was a great and personal moment, and I knew then what I know even better now: that these megalithic monuments of western Europe would exercise an irresistible fascination for me for ever.

In the same way, I shall never forget my first visit to the Dordogne and my first view of Palaeolithic art *in situ*. It was long after the Carnac megaliths had laid a spell on me; it was a year or two after the end of the 1939–45 war. My wife and I were driven from Angoulême to Les Eyzies by three women vitally interested in Palaeolithic studies: Dorothy Garrod, who was then Disney Professor of Archaeology in Cambridge, and my academical superior, and her two close friends, Suzanne de St-Mathurin and Germaine Henri-Martin. Since then Mademoiselle Henri-Martin, whose father excavated the famous Palaeolithic site of La Quina, has herself achieved fame by excavating the rock-shelter of Fontéchevade with its remains of early man, and Mademoiselle de St-Mathurin and Dorothy Garrod, now living in retirement in France, have excavated the famous rock-shelter of Angles-sur-L'Anglin, with its astonish-ing Palaeolithic carvings of animals and women. At this time these discoveries were in the future. They drove us to Les Eyzies; it was a bitterly cold March day, and my wife and I crouched in the open dickey of the car, wondering whether we were wise to go looking at caves. When we got to Lascaux, any doubts were soon dispelled. As we stood in the main entrance hall and looked round at the polychrome friezes of bulls and cows, depicted with amazing vigour and surviving to the present day with a richness of colour which is breath-taking, I was forcibly reminded of that moment in the moonlight in the Carnac alignments. The past was alive. It was no archaeological manifestation which specialist scholars could study and argue about. It was something real which everyone could understand or try to understand, something which was the beginning of their own cultural past in western Europe.

This is why I have been persuaded to write this short, intro-ductory book: to share my experiences of these great places with others. Henry Adams wrote a famous introduction to French Gothic architecture which he called *Mont St-Michel and*

Chartres, and in which he tried to get across to his readers the wonder of these places and the need to see them. It is the wonder of Carnac and Lascaux that I want to suggest, however inadequately, to readers; to tell them something of these places and, through these places, something of the early past of France.

But only the most arid and case-hardened archaeologist— and one must confess, regretfully, that such people exist—goes to France just to see megaliths and decorated caves. How fortunate that both Carnac and Lascaux are set in very beautiful parts of France. Carnac is not in that part of Brittany famed to travellers for its wild, rocky cliffs; but the Côte Sauvage of Armor does come very near to Carnac. The west side of the Quiberon Peninsula is rocky and wild—well earning the name of the Côte Sauvage; but east of that peninsula the Bay of Quiberon has a low, dune-backed coastline, and Carnac stands a mile and a half inland from the shore. The immediate countryside of Carnac is one of low hills, from the top of which you can see the sea over the pine-clad dunes. East of Carnac is the little sea that, literally, gives its name to the department in which Carnac and Quiberon are, for the name Morbihan comes from two Breton words, *mor,* sea, and *bihan,* small.

This Little Sea, the *Morbihan,* is, historically speaking, something that came into existence probably by 1000 B.C.; geologically speaking, it is very recent. At the time when the megalith-builders were flourishing in the Morbihan, the little sea was dry land, but after their time the relative levels of land and sea changed; the sea broke through the barrier of land which now survives at Locmariaquer and Port Navalo, and invaded the low-lying meadows to the north, leaving the hilltops as islands—result, the little sea with its fifty islands in its 100 square miles of area. One of my keenest memories of the south Breton countryside is of trips in little boats in the Morbihan and visits to the islanded hilltops with their prehistoric barrows like Gavr'innis and Ile Longue—that and of walks to the sea through the sweet-smelling pine woods, bathing on the sandy beaches in the moonlight and walking home along pine-needle-carpeted paths marked out by bright glow-worms.

27

INTRODUCTION

The valley of the Dordogne is full of contrast to the Morbihan coast, and when I write this I am thinking mainly of the middle Dordogne and its tributary, the Vézère—the area of the prehistoric caves. Here are deep wide valleys with lush water-meadows, the rivers edged with Lombardy poplars. The valleys are cut in limestone which produced the rock-shelters and caves for Upper Palaeolithic man's homes and temples: above them are uneven limestone plateaux. The valleys of the Dordogne and Vézère are quiet and beautiful; the rivers twist and turn along their mature, tree-shaded courses from the Central Massif of France to the sea at Bordeaux; small châteaux cling, apparently precariously, to the plateaux edges, and on the plateaux sheep wander. My most vivid memories of the Dordogne countryside are of walks in the still, summer sunshine along the gravelled, yellow, side roads on the plateaux cutting through the woods of chestnut, or of sitting underneath a road-bridge over the river and watching the poplars mirrored in the cold, fast, clear water.

I have already said that a second main reason for France is gastronomy, the food and wine which have for centuries—but not for always—made France famous, and the language of gastronomy largely French. Brittany is famous, gastronomically, for its *pré-salé* mutton, its pancakes, and, above all, its shellfish. All who love these things, and for whom a *crêperie* or the magic words *dégustation de fruits de mer* on a wall mean a tingling, salivating thrill of anticipation, will need no further advice on the delights of the Morbihan, but for those whose short holidays abroad need careful selection of the delights of past and present, let us bribe you to see the megaliths of Carnac by saying at once that here will be also oysters and lobsters and crabs and mackerel and sole, and other fishy delights, shelled and soft, until you can eat no more, and the shell mound on your plate looks like the kitchen middens which the archaeologist finds as tokens of the hunter-fishers of the Mesolithic.

The vine does not grow in the Morbihan, but in the neighbouring department of the Loire-Atlantique it flourishes, and produces one of the great French *vins de pays*, the Muscadet.

28

We in England, if we stay here and drink the wines produced by the usual wine-merchant and the usual hotel and restaurant wine list, get to know little outside the classic wines of Bordeaux, Burgundy and Champagne. The southern Burgundian wines of the Beaujolais have become more popular in recent years, perhaps since *Clochemerle*; and the north Burgundian Chablis, and the Rhône wines like Châteauneuf-du-Pape, are on many lists. But the real regional wines of France like Sancerre and Gaillac and Tavel are mysteries to the average English wine-drinker who does not travel in France. Yet a very great deal of the charm of travel in France is the discovery of the good local wine—fresh, recent, clean, and being drunk by everyone in the local café, and served in generous carafes with the market-day lunch in the local hotels. Of these local *vins de pays*, hardly ever found in London or on a London wine-merchant's list, Muscadet is one of the best. You will not find much about Muscadet in standard wine books, but in Alexis Lichine's *Wines of France* (Cassell, London, 1952), a fascinating geographical study of wine-growing in France, and much the best of recent guides to the subject, you will find this entry:

> The vineyards of Muscadet lie far down the river near the city of Nantes. They are the only classified vineyards in Brittany. All of the wine is white, and little of it is ever shipped out of the district, though some can be found in a few French restaurants. Pleasant and dry, the wines are most appealing with oysters and sea-food. Prior to the control laws, they were openly blended with Chablis, to stretch the supply of that scarce and famous wine.

Muscadet may not now be openly blended with Chablis (but something must be to give the bottles of Chablis one too often meets in England a flavour of a Pouilly-Fuissé), but something odd must happen to Muscadet itself at least on its way to England. I have never tasted a Muscadet in England that has the clean hard freshness of the wine one drinks in the Loire-Atlantique and the Morbihan. It may be that like the Beaujolais *de l'année*, that beautiful soft drink in bars and restaurants in Lyons and Mâcon, it does not travel, and has to be given an additive of a more robust wine from the middle Loire to help it on its way. It needs no help in its home, and readers can take comfort from the thought that a hard day walking over the sandy heaths of the Morbihan pursuing megaliths can always have at the end of it a *dégustation* of oysters and Muscadet.

This talk of food and wine, agreeable though it be, must not deflect us from our main purpose in this book. It is time we began our search for Palaeolithic art and megalithic monuments, but before we do so, one other word of advice. Never travel in France without proper guidebooks to hotels and restaurants. The first pre-requisite is the *Guide Michelin* (its 1963 price in England was 22*s* 6*d*), which is, in a way, the Bible of French travel. It is a mine of correct information and its ratings of restaurants and hotels beyond reproach and often inspired. The second is the *Guide des Touristes Gastronomes* now sponsored by the Kléber-Colombes organisation, published by the Editions Taride, and generally referred to nowadays as the *Guide Kléber-Colombes*. While the main part of this *Guide* is alphabetical it is prefaced by 89 departmental maps and information. The third pre-requisite is the *Guide des relais routiers*. Anyone travelling by car (and really all travellers) should become an *ami des routiers* (the London office of this organization of long-distance lorry-drivers is at 178 Fleet Street, E.C.4). The *Guide* itself costs only 17*s*, but for the additional 15*s* (plus on the first occasion the entrance fee of 10*s*) you get a discount on meals and accommodation, service station and breakdown facilities, hot and cold showers, an insurance scheme, and free legal advice. The *Guide des relais routiers* distinguishes the best eating places with the sign of the casserole. It is, we are often told, thought *chic* in France these days to be seen eating in a *relais routier*. This does not concern me: I use the *relais routiers* in France because they are good, useful, and inexpensive. Lunch in a *relais routier* will consist perhaps of *pâté* and a salad of tomatoes, a *vol au vent* of mushrooms, a steak, cheese and fruit and will cost six to nine francs. A lot of food and expensive, you may think? It is not far in advance of what you will pay in an English transport café for soup and a mixed grill, and will be so different and so much better—and better value.

INTRODUCTION

Those are the three essentials; I like to have with me also the *Guide Gastronomique de L'Auto-Journal*—it cost 8*s* 6*d* in 1963, and lists a thousand restaurants all over France where one may eat for from five to ten francs. *Les Auberges de France* issued by the Club des Auberges de France is also useful and I have always found very serviceable *Wining and Dining in France with Bon Viveur* published by Putnams in 1959. And now, guide books and manuals and maps in hand, let us turn to the Dordogne and begin our exploration of Palaeolithic art.

Getting to Lascaux and the Dordogne

Any search for Palaeolithic art must lead to the Dordogne. This is the classic area of the south French painted and engraved caves, and when one speaks of going to visit these caves the legitimate reply is: 'So you're off to the Dordogne.' The French departments which replaced the old provinces in Napoleonic times were deliberately given river names, and are organized for the most part around rivers. The old French province of Guyenne, which had Bordeaux as its capital and extended south-east to the limestone *causse* country around Rodez, was split up into six departments—namely the Gironde around Bordeaux, Lot-et-Garonne around Agen, Tarn-et-Garonne around Montauban, the Aveyron around Rodez, the Lot around Cahors, and the Dordogne, with its capital of Périgueux. The Dordogne is actually the third largest department in France.

The province of Guyenne, then, extends from the sand dunes and pines of the Landes through the vineyards of Bordeaux and the plain of the Garonne to the limestone upland country to the east that is cut through by the rivers Isle, Dordogne, Aveyron, Lot and Tarn. The limestone country to the southwest of the Central Massif and the valleys of these rivers provide some of what is, to me, the most attractive country in France, with its delightful contrasts between the barren uplands and the fertile valley bottoms. It is transitional country—transitional between the Basin of Aquitaine and the Central Massif.

1. A road in the Dordogne

2. A typical Périgord Château: the Château de la Filolie, near Montignac

Miss Freda White has written a delightful book about the countryside of three of these rivers, the Dordogne, Lot and Tarn, called *Three Rivers of France*, and this book should be read by all who think of visiting this part of France or, having visited it, want it re-created for them in prose and picture.[1]

The Gironde is the river estuary made up by the Dordogne and Garonne rivers. The Isle, on which Périgueux stands, and the Dordogne river, which gives its name to the department we are discussing, meet at Libourne. The Garonne rises in the Pyrenees and flows north-east to Toulouse, where its direction changes and it flows north-west to Bordeaux, receiving the Tarn, the Aveyron, and the Lot as tributaries as it goes. Finally, in our appreciation of the river geography of south-west France there is that curious little triangle of land which has as its base the road from Bordeaux on the Garonne to Libourne on the Dordogne, as its west side the Garonne and its east side the Dordogne, and its apex the Bec d'Ambez. North of the Bec d'Ambez is the Gironde and the sea. This triangle itself is the Mesopotamia of France, the district from which come, or from which are alleged to come—for there is still, alas! all the difference in the world between the French system of *appellation controlée* and what is actually put in your wine bottle —many of the white Bordeaux wines of an inexpensive kind sold in England.

The name Guyenne is a corruption of Aquitania. Every schoolboy is supposed to remember the words of Caesar in which Gaul is divided into three parts inhabited by the Belgae, the Aquitani and the people who called themselves Celts, but Caesar and the Romans called Gauls. All these three peoples, according to Caesar, had different languages, customs and laws. Aquitania was defined as being bounded by the Garonne, the Pyrenees and the part of the Atlantic coast nearest Spain. Gascony, the French province which is now split into the

[1] It was published by Faber and Faber in 1952 and a new edition ten years later in 1962. Another most admirable account of the Dordogne countryside is in Philip Oyler's *The Generous Earth*, first published in 1950 and now re-issued in Penguins.

departments of Landes, Basses-Pyrénées, Hautes-Pyrénées and Gers, more nearly represents the old Roman province of Aquitaine, but, however that may be, it is the country from Bordeaux east to the Central Massif that in historical times has inherited the name Aquitania and turned it into Guyenne.

Both Gascony and Guyenne are of especial interest to English travellers because they were during the twelfth and through to the fifteenth centuries the main sphere of English influence in France. In 1152 Eleanor of Aquitaine married Henri Plantagenet, who became King of England as Henry II. She brought as her dower to the English throne all Guyenne, with Gascony, Limousin and Poitou, so that for a while the King of England, already in his own right owner of Normandy, Anjou and Maine, and of Touraine and Saintonge, was really king of the whole of western France. When John succeeded to the English throne in 1199, his domains in northern France were confiscated, and Normandy, Maine, Anjou, Touraine and Poitou were recaptured by France almost without any fight. In 1259 the Treaty of Saintes left Guyenne and Gascony to Henry III of England. Up to 1360 the Black Prince was virtually King of Guyenne. Castillon, eleven miles south-east of Libourne and about eight miles from the great wine-growing town of St-Emilion, was the scene of the final defeat of the English in France in 1453. Here died the Earl of Shrewsbury, the 'Old John Talbot' of Shakespeare's *Henry VI, Part I*, 'who was so renowned in France that no man in that kingdom dared to encounter him in single combat'.

There are many strange memories of the English in France which crowd on you as you travel around. One of the strangest of all is the famous Abbey of Fontevrault, not far from Saumur and Chinon in the Touraine. This abbey has all sorts of curiosities—it had two communities, one for men and the other for women, and for many years the two communities were ruled over by an abbess; it has a magnificent church and one of the few surviving examples of a Romanesque kitchen; it is today in the unusual position of half belonging to the Beaux-Arts and being preserved as a national monument for visitors, while the other half is a prison. The visitors walk through lines of prisoners setting out for work or returning from the fields, as they make for the great Romanesque church. Inside this church are the tombs of Henry II, his wife, Eleanor of Aquitaine, and their son Richard Cœur de Lion. The effigy of Henry II is the most ancient of any English king. It should make a difficult question in any guessing game: 'What English King is buried in a site most of which is now a French prison?'

Another memory of the English struggle in France is preserved in all wine lists. The Château Talbot, which is a fourth growth of the Médoc, dates back to the fifteenth century and is named after the old Earl of Shrewsbury who lost the Battle of Castillon and so ended the English domination of Aquitaine. Whenever I drink this fine claret, I think sentimentally of this sad occasion—sad for the English, but perhaps not for the French. The connexion between the Bordeaux wine-merchants and England was very close, and is reflected in the wine trade that still survives between Bordeaux and the western ports of Britain. This trade goes right back to Roman times. In his *History of Europe* H. A. L. Fisher gives a vivid parallel between the English in Guyenne in the twelfth to the fifteenth centuries and the British in India: 'The English then thought it just as natural to be at Bordeaux', he wrote in 1930, 'as they today find it natural to be in Bombay; the people of Bordeaux thought it as little natural as do today the people of Bombay.'

A third memory of the English domination of Guyenne will often be met with as you travel about in the Dordogne country. In the thirteenth century the frontier between Guyenne and the Languedoc was fought over during the Albigensian War, called after Albi, where the Albigensian heresy arose in the twelfth century. This heresy was condemned in 1165, but violent measures began only after the Papal Legate was murdered in 1208. Then Pope Innocent III ordered the Albigensian Crusade, which was led by Simon de Montfort and was, historians claim, the bloodiest massacre in medieval history. In 1210 Simon de Montfort took Béziers and had 20,000 of its inhabitants massacred without any mercy. He was egged on to this by the Abbot of Cîteaux and the Bishop of Montpellier; the Abbot, when the crusading soldiers hesitated whom to kill, is said to have cried out the biblical words: Kill them all; for the Lord knoweth them that are His (2 Tim. ii. 19.)[1] As a consequence of this Albigensian War, fortress towns were built by the English in Guyenne; they are all on a rectangular plan with streets at right angles and an arcaded central space, and were known as *bastides*. There are very good examples of these *bastides* in the Dordogne. Monpazier is one; it was built by Edward I in 1284.[2]

The English legacy in the Dordogne is not merely *bastides* and the Black Prince. Many English names survive, and antiquities of various kinds are still ascribed to the English. I myself had a curious experience in the Aveyron in 1939. I was looking for a chambered long barrow near Rodez, and could not get anyone to understand what sort of field antiquity I was looking for, or to recognize it when I had at last fully described it. In the end a look of comprehension dawned on the face of a farmer and he said, 'Ah, monsieur, vous cherchez le tombeau des Anglais.' The English occupation of the twelfth to the fifteenth centuries had in south French history come to have the sort of role which Caesar and the Romans occupy in English history. But it was a quaint reminder of the times of the Black Prince to have prehistoric monuments called the Englishmen's grave just as we in England call prehistoric monuments Caesar's Camp or the Danes' Camp.

In France there are not only departmental and province names to remember, but also *pays* names—the names of geographical regions or districts. We use these sorts of names in England when we refer to the Cotswolds, or the Weald, or the Peak district. In France there are very many *pays* names, and they are very widely used. In the region of south-west France which concerns us here, there are three *pays* names that are

[1] Quoted by Caesarius of Heisterbach in 'Of Demons', *The Dialogue on Miracles*, Vol. I, p. 343 (*Broadway Medieval Library* ed. G. G. Coulton and Eileen Power).

[2] In England, Winchelsea is an imperfect example of a *bastide*.

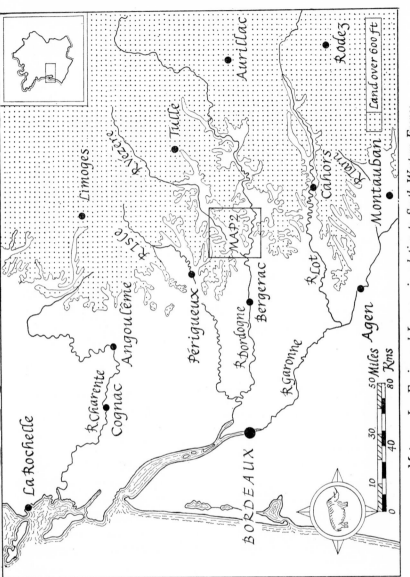

Map 1. *Les Eyzies and Lascaux in relation to South-Western France*

constantly cropping up—Périgord, Quercy and Rouergue. The Rouergue is the country around Rodez which today, very approximately, forms the department of the Aveyron; everyone will remember the brilliant and classic portrait of a Rouergue farm in the film *Farrebique*. Quercy is nowadays represented by the department of Lot around its splendid town of Cahors, while the department of Tarn-et-Garonne around Montauban is Haut Quercy.[1] Périgord is nowadays represented by the Dordogne department, itself centred on Périgueux, but extends southwards into the Lot-et-Garonne around Agen. There are actually two smaller *pays* names in use: the Périgord Blanc, which is to the north of Périgueux, and the Périgord Noir, which is to the south, extending from Bergerac to Sarlat—it is so called because of the deep shadow cast by the trees over the high plateau. It is this Périgord Noir country with which we are concerned in our search for the classic sites of Palaeolithic art, and particularly that part of it between the rivers Vézère and Dordogne extending eastwards to the road from Montignac to Sarlat (*see* Maps 1 and 2).

The River Dordogne rises in the Central Massif of France in the Puy de Sancy and flows through the spas of Mont-Dore and La Bourboule and then south-westwards to the sea west of Libourne. Its main tributary is the Vézère, which rises in the Limousin country near Ussel and joins the Dordogne at a charming little hamlet called Limeuil, some fifteen miles east of Bergerac. It is the winding valley of the Vézère from Montignac to Les Eyzies that concerns us particularly, and is the classic area of French prehistory. Les Eyzies-de-Tayac is about five miles north-east of Limeuil, and Montignac a farther ten miles to the north-east. All the sites we have come to the Dordogne to see are really in this ten-mile stretch of country from Les Eyzies-de-Tayac to Montignac, in the middle of the Périgord Noir, in the middle of the department of the Dordogne, in the middle of Guyenne—right in the middle of Aquitaine.

[1] The origin of the word Quercy is disputed, some authors deriving it from *quercus*, the Latin for oak tree, others from the Celtic tribe, the *Cadurci*, who occupied the area in pre-Roman and Roman times.

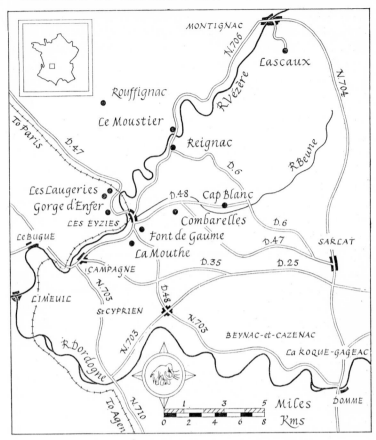

Map 2. Main Prehistoric sites in the Dordogne

First, how to get there? There are really two centres. Les Eyzies and Montignac. You can stay at either, or both. My strong advice is to stay entirely, or at first, at Les Eyzies, where you can first see the sites that made the Dordogne classic in world archaeology, and then, and then only, go to see Lascaux, which is near Montignac. I would insist on this advice even for those people who are motoring from the north and come from Limoges on N.20 or from Clermont Ferrand on N.89. Coming this way you will pass through Montignac and be urged to visit the Grotte de Lascaux. Resist all temptation; go on to Les

39

Eyzies and first see La Mouthe, Font de Gaume and Les Combarelles: then drive the ten miles back to Montignac for Lascaux. Lascaux is so much better preserved than the other sites, so well *amenagé* by the French, and is really so much the highlight of a visit to the Dordogne to see Palaeolithic art, that it should be reserved for the final visit.

Les Eyzies is a village, Montignac a small town. Both are agreeable to stay in, but it is perfectly easy, with a car, to stay anywhere else in the Périgord Noir when visiting the caves—Beynac-et-Cazenac or La Roque-Gageac, two villages wonderfully situated on the Dordogne in what is perhaps the most beautiful reach of that most beautiful river, or Domme, splendidly situated on top of a hill just south of the Dordogne, or the little town of Sarlat. But for me, any proper or serious visit to the caves demands a stay at Les Eyzies.

It is quite easy to get to Les Eyzies by train from Paris. You can leave Paris-Austerlitz at 8.40, arriving at Limoges at 13.2; after a quarter of an hour's wait, another train takes you on, bringing you to Périgueux at 15.5. A third-class autorail, leaving Périgueux at 15.42, delivers you at Les Eyzies at 16.22 in time for your five o'clock tea, your *apéritif*, and a walk along the river before you eat your first Périgord dinner. A later train leaves Paris in the summer at 12.40 (admirably arranged for those who have come overnight or travelled by early morning aircraft), and gets you to Les Eyzies at 19.10. For those who have travelled to Paris during the day from England a night train leaves Paris at 21.50, getting you to Les Eyzies next morning at 7.53, while in the summer there is a special night train leaving Paris at 22.25 and depositing you at Les Eyzies at 6.5 in the morning. Les Eyzies happens to be on the main Paris-Limoges-Périgueux-Agen line, and at least one of the night trains has *couchette* sleeping accommodation. It is thus very easy to get to Les Eyzies from London within less than twenty-four hours. Flying to Bordeaux, you can get there even more quickly, but, either way, aircraft to Paris or Bordeaux enable you to dine in Les Eyzies.

From 30th September 1962, the S.N.C.F. have announced a

new service to the Dordogne: Paris-Périgueux at 112 kilometres an hour. This is effected by *autorail rapide* first class from Limoges to Périgueux which connects with the *train rapide Le Capitole*. One can now leave Paris at 17.45 arriving at Thiviers at 21.49 and Périgueux at 22.13. The return journey can be done leaving Périgueux at 19.24 and arriving in Paris at midnight.

Montignac is not so easy to reach. The main line from Paris to Toulouse passes through the junction of Brive-la-Gaillarde on the Vézère. The *rapide* leaving Paris-Austerlitz at 12.40 gets to Brive at 18.13; a ten-minute wait and then the second-class express SB takes you on to Condat-le-Lardin in twenty minutes, and from here a bus delivers you at Montignac at four minutes past nine.[1] A railway is marked on the Michelin map—and it is essential to have the Michelin sheet 75 for your travels in the Dordogne—from Brive to Sarlat and via Montignac, but no time-table announces trains running on this line. Communication from Les Eyzies to Montignac is not very easy, but can be achieved by bus and train, and in the height of the season— that is, from early July to the end of September—there are special tourist buses connecting these two centres.

While it is easy to get to the Dordogne caves by train and easy to see the caves from Les Eyzies and Montignac without a car—the distances involved are not great, there are a few buses, and bicycles can be hired—any visit to this country will be immeasurably more delightful by car, and you will have the added pleasure of driving across France to the Dordogne and back again. By road there are many ways across France to the Périgord Noir, and I have done all of them at various times. The selection of a route really depends on the point of entry into France. I suppose most people will land with their cars by air

---

[1] I take all these times from the current edition of the *Indicateur Chaix*, the fine French time-table. This French *Bradshaw* is simplicity itself to work, with its maps and numbered trains. All the Les Eyzies-Montignac information is in section 4 *Sud-Ouest*, and the relevant tables are 440, 450, 454, 455 and 4315. I have been using the 1962–3 edition; all these times should be checked with the French Railway Office in Piccadilly. It is essential, of course, to use the twenty-four-hour clock system in dealing with Continental trains and time-tables.

at Calais or Le Touquet or by boat at Calais, Dunkirk, Boulogne or Dieppe. From these northern ports to the Dordogne there are roughly speaking three routes or bands of routes: the eastern, keeping to the east of Paris; the central, going straight through Paris; and the western, keeping to the west of Paris. The central route is the shortest; it is what is known as the *Route Mauve* from Paris to the Pyrenees. The *Route Mauve* takes in many roads which leave Paris to Orleans as N.20, then divides, N.20 going on directly via Châteauroux and Limoges, while just to the east of it is N.140 from Gien through Bourges, Guéret and Tulle. These two main roads to the south lead you easily and quickly to the Dordogne—you can strike right across country from Limoges to Les Eyzies and Montignac or approach them from Périgueux or Brive.

This *Route Mauve* is a lovely way to get to the Dordogne. Why is it called this? 'Simply because this tone dominates, from the undergrowth of the Sologne to the violet-tinted slopes of the Pyrenees, passing through the heather of the Limousin, the lavender fields of the Quercy and the violets of Toulouse'.[1] If you choose this central route, use N.140 so that you can linger on the shores of the Loire at Gien or Sully or Briare with a glass of Sancerre or Pouilly Fumé in your hands, and so that you can sit looking at the sun coming through the incomparably richly coloured windows of Bourges Cathedral.

The western route to the Dordogne from the Channel ports goes through Rouen and Chartres, or, sweeping even farther west through Alençon and Le Mans, comes down through Tours, Poitiers and Angoulême. This is the way I have most often arrived in the Dordogne, and to me it is always associated with the great moment in driving south through France when you cross or feel you have crossed the line from the Langue d'Oil of the north to the Langue d'Oc of the south. The boundary is approximately the 46 degrees north parallel, which on this route cuts the Poitiers-Angoulême road somewhere between Ruffec and Mansle. But it is at Angoulême and south of Angou-

---

[1] I quote from that excellent magazine *The Traveller in France* issued by the French Tourist Office.

lême that I feel I am moving into the south; there is a sudden clarity in the air, the sky is bluer, the soil is the yellow brown which my mind's eye associates with Provence, and the *tuiles* of Provence are already on the gently pitched roofs. We are already well south of the northern limits of vine cultivation and of the cultivation of maize; we are, admittedly, north of the limits of mulberry and olive, but as we drive along the ridge road from Angoulême to Périgueux we are really in the south.

The eastern route seems perhaps at first sight out of the way, but it is not so for those who land at Calais or Dunkirk. They can leave Paris to the right and go down through Burgundy and then across the Central Massif through Clermont Ferrand. This route has great advantages; first of all north Burgundy with lovely towns like Semur-en-Auxois to be visited, and Vézelay and Autun, and a host of brilliant restaurants like the Côte d'Or at Saulieu and the Hôtel de la Gare at Montbard—and those who travel in France and do not know Alexandre Dumaine at Saulieu and André Belin at Montbard will have missed some of the great delights and triumphs of French cookery. Then, after Burgundy, the route across the Central Massif—the valley of the Allier, Clermont Ferrand, the geographical delights of driving to the top of the Puy-de-Dôme and the archaeological delights of the great Auvergnat Romanesque churches at Issoire and Brioude and Orcival. And, after the Auvergne, across to Périgord; one summer I went through the Cantal country because I have such a high opinion of the Cantal cheese—so reminiscent of Caerphilly and Wensleydale —and wanted to see the high mountain pastures and the *burons* where the cheese is made by the transhumants during the summer. We went through the tunnel of the Lioran, leaving to the east the pine-clad slopes of the Allagnon, and came out to the west into the oak and chestnut of the Cère; with the Plomb de Cantal on our left we motored down through Aurillac and then took N.673 to St-Céré and Bretenoux, a mile or two to the west of which the Cère flows into the Dordogne. We stayed the night at Sousceyrac at a small village inn which has the publicity advantage of being called Au Déjeuner de Sousceyrac. It was a wonderful introduction to the Périgord cuisine, and we felt we were already in the Dordogne. It turned out to be a nine-course dinner: *potage, foie gras maison, truite meunière, cèpes paysanne, tournedos, salade, fromages, omelette surprise,* and then strawberries. 'Would that do?' asked Madame. If not, there were the additional specialities of *confit d'oie chaud* or *confit de dinde mayonnaise,* but those would demand supplementary payments. And the price in this mid-century moment of 1962? Nineteen shillings. I gave Madame Prunet, who runs this unpretentious little inn, full marks for her *foie gras* and full marks for her *cèpes paysanne*: so often these fungi come to the table in a fleshy condition that is near to being uncooked. Hers were crisp and fresh, well-cooked and well-garlicked, and next morning she told me the secret of her method of cooking *cèpes*. We set off down into the Dordogne with the best possible introduction to the gastronomy of that region, and followed the Dordogne down to Souillac and Sarlat and past Domme to St-Cyprien and then over the hill into the Vézère Valley and Les Eyzies.

I do not know now which way I shall next go to the Dordogne, all the routes across France are so agreeable, but fortunately you go and return, so there are always two routes to try. Those landing their car by air at Cherbourg or by boat at St-Malo will naturally take the western route to Tours and Poitiers.[1]

Last summer I drove from north Burgundy south through St-Pourçain (so that I could degust on the spot this very interesting white wine) and Vichy (for the *vrai crème Vichyssoise* at Le Patio Albert Ier) and Riom, so that I could visit at Mozac the Eglise de Notre-Dame du Marthuret with its *vierge à l'oiseau* and the *vierge noire* (I hope like myself you are a connoisseur of black virgins) and on to St-Céré through Bort-les-Orgues and Argentat. Another way would be through Tulle and Brive. I have never stayed or eaten in Tulle but all my friends who have warmly praise La Toque Blanche with its *écrevisses au sancerre, noisette d'agneau aux herbes flanquée de cèpes,* and its *crêpes flambées.*

[1] The two Michelin special maps, *De Paris aux Pyrénées* and *Paris—Le Midi par L'Auvergne,* are most valuable for planning your journey across France to the Dordogne.

I shall take this route another time. Last year I fetched up for the night at the Hôtel Central at Bort-les-Orgues, at the headwaters of the river Dordogne and just below the great dam. My wife and I slept happily in a beautifully modernized bedroom despite the mass of water dammed up above us and a tremendous September fair in the market-place—where the Dutch army on manoeuvres nearby were shattering the faith of the rifle-stall holders in the law of averages and accurately sharpshooting their way to win ducks, geese, teddy bears and bottles of *pelure d'oignon*.

I warmly recommend the Hôtel Central. It has been reorganized in the Logis de France scheme, and its proprietor-chef-director, Monsieur Lacombe, believes in a visible kitchen and looks out rather disdainfully at his greedy clients eating his specialities. And there are a lot of specialities—*quenelle de coulis d'écrevisses sauce nantua, escalopine de veau à la façon du chef* (with cream and mushrooms but the rich cream sauce dried away with vermouth), and a most marvellous *gratinée au porto*—a remarkable *soupe à l'oignon* to end all such soups—full of cream, garlic, port—a meal in itself.

We lunched the next day—Sunday—at Argentat between the Massif Central and the Dordogne. All our books recommended warmly two places, the Hôtel Gilbert and the Hôtel Fouillade. We chose the latter because it was on a square (the Place Gambetta) and looked really bourgeois—and is there anything more rewarding and exciting than partaking of the French bourgeois Sunday lunch out? This was rewarding. The meal was *melon au porto, langoustines mayonnaise, ris de veau*, a *gigot* with *pommes de terre dauphine*, cheeses and a *baba au rhum*. This quite excellent six-course lunch cost, without wine, thirteen shillings and sixpence (September, 1962). Very difficult to beat anywhere. We certainly drove on to Les Eyzies in a very happy frame of mind.

It is not a personal idiosyncrasy of mine to suppose that the Dordogne is one of the most agreeable areas of France—and therefore of the world—in which to eat. In his excellent *Bouquet de France* (1952), Samuel Chamberlain says: 'There can be no doubt about it: Périgord is one of the regions in France where one dines best of all.' It is the region where truffles and *foie gras* —the livers of the giant Toulouse goose—abound. It is the region where, though there is of course butter, pork fat, olive oil and walnut oil, the cooking is based on the yellow goose fat. (The area comes in Waverley Root's 'Domain of Fat' which includes Alsace-Lorraine, the Central Plateau and Languedoc.)[1] The great dishes are great indeed: *ballotine de dinde* (the white meat of turkey stuffed with *foie gras*), *truffes sous la cendre, tourtes de truffes à la périgourdine* (a pie filled with truffles and *foie gras* doused in brandy), *oeufs en cocotte à la périgourdine* (eggs broken over a layer of *foie gras* and cooked in a casserole with *sauce périgourdine*), *confit d'oie* (particularly *à la sarladaise*, that is to say served with sliced potatoes and truffles fried in goose fat), *cou farci*, and *cèpes* in any form.

The original version of *truffes sous la cendre* consists of seasoned spiced truffles sprinkled with brandy wrapped in a thin slice of salt pork and then in heavy paper and tucked in to the ashes of a fire. The version of this classic dish which I had in the Grand Hôtel at Souillac was first packed in *foie gras* before the salt pork, and the whole wrapped into a square of dough and cooked in an oven. One of the most memorable and great dishes of the world.

The vineyards of the Dordogne are not as distinguished as the food. They are a continuation of the vineyards of Bordeaux. There are 90,000 acres under vines, 35,000 growers and an output of between 9 and 27 million gallons a year. Among the Dordogne wines there is Monbazillac of course—light, sweet, delicate, high in alcohol, straightforward. Other regional white wines include Brantôme, Coteaux de Périgueux, Côtes de

---

[1] Waverley Root's *The Food of France* was first published in America in 1958, and the following year in London. Samuel Chamberlain's *Bouquet de France*, subtitled 'An Epicurean Tour of the French Provinces' was published in New York and London in 1952. Other books to use, apart from the annual guides, are Jean Conil, *Gastronomic Tour de France* (London, 1959), Elizabeth David, *French Provincial Cooking* (London, 1960), and Curnonsky's *Traditional Recipes of the Provinces of France* (London, 1961)—an English adaptation of *Recettes des Provinces de France*, first edited by P. E. Lamaison.

Saussignac, Château des Granges, Marsalet. Among the reds
are Pecharmant and Monsaquel (both from Bergerac), Château
de Panisseau, Brantôme and Montazeau—all light and delicate with a good taste, powerful but with little nose. Some *rosé*
wines are made around Bergerac. There is actually a white
appellation contrôlée of Rouffignac (Chapter VI).

With all these good dishes and wines in our mind, where do
we stay when we get to the Dordogne? Montignac with its
2,000 inhabitants has several hotels, one very good, the Soleil
d'Or. It has 33 rooms from 8 to 16 francs. The meals are 7.50
or 10 francs. I have never stayed there but know many people
who have and have been more than satisfied. I have lunched
there—it was a good generous lunch—excellent value for money.
I am much attracted by a little restaurant hotel opened up
two miles away from Montignac at Aubas; it is called L'Arzème
and is run by Monsieur and Madame Chevalier. It has a
swimming pool and peace and quiet. I have never done more
than swim and drink there but the menus look very interesting.

South of Montignac and half-way between Sarlat and Les
Eyzies is the Hostellerie Delibie-Veyret at Marquay. I have
lunched excellently here on several occasions on its shaded
terrasse: I would think it a delightful place to stay for those who
want peace and the quiet interest of village life. It has only
ten rooms at 10 francs each; the meals are 7 and 10 francs (with
wine and service included).

But most people will stay in Les Eyzies itself. There are four
hotels: Les Glycines, the Cro-Magnon, the Centre and the
Poste. The Glycines and Cro-Magnon are of the same standard
each with 25 to 30 rooms with full *pension* from £2 10s to £3 a
day and their gastronomic meals 13 to 15 francs s.t.c. (i.e. *ser-
vices et taxes compris*, in a word, all-inclusive rates). The Poste has
18 rooms but is building on more; the full *pension* rates are under
£2 a day. I looked through the menus last summer while
sipping an *apéritif* and being tantalized by the delicious cooking
smells coming out of the kitchen. The proprietor has put a
sarcastic little notice outside his restaurant saying 'Ici l'hôtel
sans étoiles'. The Poste is shut for a fortnight in October, the

Glycines and Cro-Magnon are closed from November to the end of February. The fourth hotel, the Hôtel du Centre, is open all the year round. It is in the middle of the village, has 11 rooms and its *pension* charges are £2 and under a day.

I am prejudiced in favour of Les Glycines and go back there year after year with great anticipations of pleasure which are always fulfilled. It is the oldest hotel and very well run. The cuisine produces all the things that you expect a good cook to do in the Dordogne, and all very well, from a simple *omelette aux truffes* to *sauce périgourdine* and *beignets*. The vegetable cooking is of the highest standard and as I write my thoughts crowd with memories of *épinards à la crème, fonds d'artichauts clamart* or *mornay* and *champignons à la provençale* eaten there. I fell in love with this hotel when I first went there: sentiment, my friendship with the proprietors and the excellence of the cooking will keep me going back there while time, energy and money last. It is where I shall go for my convalescence, sitting on the terrace in the sun, listening to the noise of the sawmill, a glass of Monbazillac or Pecharmant in my hand, wondering what delights I am next going to be given to eat.

Prejudice and preference should be fairly declared and I have done so. Let me also quote what Waverley Root says in his *The Food of France* (p. 467): 'Les Glycines and the Cro-Magnon, both devoted to presenting local dishes and wines. I would rate the first as a slightly better buy, but the difference is not great and you might very well reverse my preference.' Les Glycines was started in 1862 by the Lesvignes family, and last summer my wife and I had the pleasure of raising a glass in celebration of its centenary to Madame Lesvignes-Duclaud, the grand-daughter of the house, and Jacqueline, her daughter, and her hard-working son-in-law, Marcel Pialat, who do not spare themselves in maintaining a tradition of friendly and efficient hospitality and excellent cooking.

But it is time we left our hotel terraces and set out to see Les Eyzies and begin our initiation into Palaeolithic art.

3. (b) stuffing geese

3. Food in the Dordogne: (a) the nut cracker

4. Les Eyzies

✤ III ✤

Les Eyzies

As you walk away from your hotel along the main road you will see what a very small place Les Eyzies is. About 500 people live in the village itself, and a total of 1,100 formally within the confines of the commune. The village is situated at the confluence of the Beune and the Vézère, although there is no dramatic joining of two streams, as there is at Limeuil, where Vézère and Dordogne join. You have to go scrambling past back gardens and half-hearted attempts at riverside cafés and across a meadow to find the Beune, its flow controlled by sluices, trickling into the swift-flowing Vézère. The valley of the Vézère here at Les Eyzies is a smaller-scale example of the classic and characteristic Dordogne Valley not far away—flat valley bottom flanked by steep valley walls formed by limestone cliffs, and the upland plateau tops either sand-capped and forested or barren limestone.

The limestone cliffs rise steeply, sometimes sheer, from the river edge to heights of between 150 and nearly 300 feet. The plateau surface of the Périgord Noir country, in the middle of which stands Les Eyzies, is roughly 600 to 750 feet above sea-level. That is the essential physical characteristic of this country-side—the plateau seamed by the broad, flat, steep-sided valleys of the Dordogne and Vézère. These river valleys are about 90 to 100 feet above sea-level, and the river-courses meander about on the valley bottoms, giving alternately sharply undercut cliff-surfaces with overhanging rocks or sloping sides away from the river.

The rock everywhere is a yellowish Cretaceous limestone,

D   49

while the plateau surface is in parts capped by ferruginous sands and gravels. At the present day the limestone plateau surfaces bear white oak, hornbeam, juniper scrub, box and evergreen oak; the plateau sands have the chestnut forests mixed with black oaks and an undergrowth of gorse and bracken which gave rise to the name Périgord Noir. The rock surfaces bear ferns, mosses, lichens, evergreen oaks and ivy; the river banks are fringed by alder and willow and whenever there is water in the valley bottoms Lombardy poplars grow. The landscape picture that remains in the mind's eye is one of poplars in the wide river meadows, and of steep, overhanging limestone cliffs leading up to the limestone plateaux. An impression of this memorable and characteristic countryside can be obtained from the photographs reproduced here (Frontispiece and Plate 1).

It is to these limestone cliffs that Les Eyzies owes its present fame, which enables tourist pamphlets to describe it as 'The Capital of Prehistory', and made the great French historian Camille Julian say of it: 'Tout Français qui a le culte de ses ancêtres, tout homme qui a la curiosité respectueuse de son passé, doit faire le pélerinage des Eyzies.' These limestone cliffs not only overhang, but are pitted with caves; horizontal grooves in the limestone start the process of cave-making. The overhanging cliffs and the caves have been used by man as dwelling-places since the end of the Ice Age. They provided some of the houses of Upper Palaeolithic man just as they provided houses in the Middle Ages and right up to the present day. Plate 4 of Les Eyzies village shows modern houses built up against the cliff walls, with the naked limestone acting sometimes as back wall, sometimes as roof, and often as both. Horizontal grooves are cut in the rock just above the roofs to prevent the water trickling down the cliff face and coming into the houses. As the Upper Palaeolithic rock-shelters must date back to 20,000 B.C. and even earlier, the little village of Les Eyzies can claim to be one of the oldest occupied sites in France, although, of course, this does not mean that the occupation has been continuous from the Ice Age to the Atomic Age.

The discovery of the antiquity of Les Eyzies, like the discovery of the antiquity of man himself, is a comparatively recent matter. In Augustus Hare's *South-Western France*, published in 1890, we find the following entry:

> *Les Eyzies* (a humble hotel near the station). In this neighbourhood is a group of the most remarkable caverns in France. Very near the station is the entrance to the *Grotte de Cro-Magnon* of the third prehistoric age, where five prehistoric skeletons have been found entire . . . at 7 k. N.E. is the *Grotte de la Madeleine* of the fourth prehistoric period, where an ivory tablet was found engraved with a representation of a mammoth. At 11 k. is the *Grotte du Moustier*, which has given the name of Mousterienne to the first prehistoric period.

Augustus Hare was still very close to the original discoveries, and his phrases about the prehistoric periods are not quite accurate, but he is beginning to convey the excitement of the discoveries in the Dordogne to the general travelling public.

A few years later the discoveries are in Baedeker. In the fifth edition of Karl Baedeker's *Guidebook for Travellers in Southern France* (published in 1907) we find this entry describing the journey from Périgueux to Tarbes:

> *Les Eyzies*, a picturesquely placed village, surrounded and overhung by magnificent rocks. These contain a large number of *Grottos*, where remarkable discoveries of bones of extinct animals, human skeletons and implements of flint and reindeer horn have been made.

There are two interesting points about this entry of fifty years ago. First, the English translator has given the wrong impression by using the word *Grottos*; it is a mistranslation of the French word *grottes*, which means a cave or a rock-shelter. The archaeological sites which are of such interest to us and which have brought us to this part of France are all called *grotte* in France; the Grotte de Lascaux, for example, or the Grotte de Combarelles and the Grotte de Font de Gaume; and these are all caves (the French word *caves* means, of course, 'cellars'). They are natural caves, often extending deeply into the limestone hillsides of the country, which were utilized by man. But not all *grottes* are interesting archaeologically or were used by man. The Grotte de Carpe Diem and the Grotte du Grand Roc, for example, to which visitors to Les Eyzies are constantly being urged, are caves with no evidence of human occupation. They are famous for their natural beauties—for the stalactites and crystallizations which often resemble growths of coral.

The visitor to Les Eyzies should certainly see these strange, impressive natural beauties if he has time, but we are concerned with the caves that have been used by man. Broadly speaking, these are of two kinds: the deep caves to which the term *grotte* is more properly reserved, and the rock-shelters for which the French usually use the word *abri*. The rock-shelters or *abris* are merely low, overhanging rocks protecting a shelf in the rock; the *grottes* are deep caves. There is also a very considerable difference in the utilization of these sites by prehistoric man. The *grottes* or deep caves were used for special magico-religious purposes; while the rock-shelters or *abris* were dwelling sites.[1] Of course, this is a general distinction for convenience of description.

The second interesting point in the Baedeker entry which I have quoted is the absence of any reference to the existence of painted and engraved caves; yet this was the edition of 1907. It is surprising that there should be no reference to Font de Gaume, to Les Combarelles and La Mouthe in 1907, but to see the perspective from which the Baedeker notes were then written we must look briefly at the history of the discovery of Upper Palaeolithic art. Until the beginning of the nineteenth century, few people had any clear idea of the great antiquity of man, and most thought of man's past in terms of perhaps 6,000 years. Archbishop Ussher had calculated that the earth and man had been created in 4004 B.C., and this date was printed in the margins of the Authorized Version of the Bible. The nineteenth century saw the development of stratigraphical

---

[1] In addition to the distinction between *grottes* and *abris*, the archaeological tourist in the Dordogne should get used to the word *gisement*, which French archaeologists use for the stratified accumulation of debris on the site of a prehistoric settlement. *Abris* have *gisements*; *grottes* hardly ever do so.

geology and the belief that the deposition of all the observable superimposed strata or layers must have taken a very long time; it was assumed that these layers could not have been formed any more quickly than the rate at which present-day lakes and rivers form mud and sand deposits. This belief in uniformitarianism lies at the basis of the new geology of the early nineteenth century; the new geology lies at the basis of the new archaeology—namely, prehistory: if you accepted these geological views, the record of the rocks could not have been the result of a catastrophe like the Noachian deluge.

The nineteenth century also saw the development of an archaeological theory which postulated technological stages in the cultural development of man before the age of iron in which we now live and were living in the nineteenth century. The Danish archaeologist C. J. Thomsen postulated an age of Stone and an age of Bronze before the Iron Age, and stratigraphy in the Danish bogs and Swiss lakes showed this succession to be chronologically correct. This classification of the prehistoric past was elaborated; the present elaborate table for France has already been set out in Chapter I (p.24). The classification was popularized in England by Sir John Lubbock—later Lord Avebury, whose *Prehistoric Times* was published in 1865. It was Lubbock who proposed the names Palaeolithic and Neolithic for the divisions of the Stone Age into Old Stone Age and New Stone Age. At that time the Palaeolithic was thought of in terms of chipped stone tools; the Neolithic, of polished stone tools and pottery. This broad distinction has more fundamental differences; the Palaeolithic was the era of food-gathering hunters and fishers and lasted for thousands of years—indeed, for perhaps 90 per cent of man's time on earth—whereas the Neolithic was the era of the first peasant villagers in Europe, the first farms with domesticated animals and cultivated grain.

Traces of Palaeolithic man—the skeletal traces of his body and the archaeological traces of his culture in the shape of stone tools—were found associated with extinct animals and deep down in deposits that must have taken a long time to form, if we accepted the principles of uniformitarianism. All these

53

facts, together with the general acceptance of the doctrine of organic evolution following the publication of Darwin's *Origin of Species*, meant that man had a very long past: well before 4004 B.C. Archaeologists then set about studying the remains that could be ascribed to this long Palaeolithic past. Much of this work was done in France, and many of the names given to the stages of the Palaeolithic are French. Some of the early tools of man were found in the river gravels of the Somme at places like Chelles, Abbeville and St-Acheul, and these sites have given their names to some of the early stages of what is usually called the Lower Palaeolithic—namely, the Abbevillian (or Chellean, as it used to be called) and the Acheulian. These two stages or cultures of the Lower Palaeolithic do not concern us in the Dordogne, but the later stages of the Palaeolithic do.

In the 'sixties of last century a Frenchman by the name of Edouard Lartet explored caves in the Ariège, Haute-Garonne and Tarn-et-Garonne departments of southern France. Lartet was a magistrate who abandoned the study of law for that of palaeontology and archaeology. He first studied fossil animals and then turned to the cultural fossils of man—the earliest stone tools. In 1852 a French peasant called Bonnemaison was mending the road near Aurignac in the Haute-Garonne; he put his hand into a rabbit hole and drew out a human bone. Interested in this curious discovery, he dug down and found a great slab of rock closing the mouth of a rock-shelter. Behind this, in a cavity, were seventeen human skeletons, with the remains of extinct animals, flint and ivory tools and engravings on bones. The Mayor of Aurignac decided that these remains should be given Christian burial, and these seventeen Palaeolithic skeletons were reinterred in the cemetery nearby. No one seemed much interested in this discovery until Edouard Lartet heard of it. He re-examined the cave and decided that the tools of flint, bone and ivory were those of Palaeolithic man. He went on with the examination of other caves and rock-shelters in the Pyrenees, and while he was engaged in this work he was sent by a collector of fossils in the Périgord a box of flint and bone splinters from a cave at Les Eyzies, with the information that the caves of the Périgord abounded in these things. Lartet transferred his attentions to the valley of the Vézère. From 1863 onwards, helped financially and scientifically by an English banker friend, Henry Christy, he began a series of excavations at sites in the valley of the Vézère. In 1862-3 he was digging at Laugerie Haute and Les Eyzies and La Madeleine and Gorge d'Enfer. At the same time another Frenchman, the Marquis de Vibraye, began excavating Laugerie Basse. The results of the Lartet excavations were published in London in 1865 in a large work called *Reliquiae Aquitanicae*.[1]

From then on Les Eyzies became one of the centres of Palaeolithic research. Discoveries followed each other, and soon it was not only tools that had been found there, but man himself, and, later still, decorated caves. The story of the decorated caves must wait for the next chapter, when we will visit the classic sites. These discoveries of man's temples came after the discovery of his burial customs. In 1868 the road from Les Eyzies to Sarlat was being constructed, and the contractors cut into the rock-shelter of Cro-Magnon. Here, in what is now the garage of the Hôtel Cro-Magnon, they discovered some flint tools and skeletons. Lartet's son, Louis, was sent for, and he excavated the rock-shelter, showing that it had contained the burials of three individuals. These were the first burials ever found of Upper Palaeolithic man—for the Aurignac skeletons, although at the time Lartet did not know it, were Neolithic in date—and they were studied with the greatest of care by the French physical anthropologist Broca. On the basis of his work he defined and described Cro-Magnon man. The interest was not only that of a new physical type—the type of man who made the Upper Palaeolithic tools and lived in the rock-shelters. It was also the fact that these were careful, deliberate burials.

The Les Eyzies area had then produced not only well-authenticated living sites, but burial-places, and Upper Palaeolithic man. It was soon to produce proof of the magic and reli-

---

[1] Half of what Lartet and Christy found can be seen in the British Museum; the other half is at St-Germain-en-Laye.

gion of Upper Palaeolithic man. Small wonder, then, it was soon claimed as the Capital of Prehistory. Small wonder too, that, with so many discoveries made in the region, the rock-shelters should have given their names to so many divisions of the Upper Palaeolithic. It is quite a shock to the amateur or professional archaeologist when he first comes to the Dordogne with his mind accustomed to names like Mousterian, Tayacian, Magdalenian, Micoquian and to speak of Cro-Magnon man, and then sees the Hôtel Cro-Magnon, and signposts to La Madeleine, La Micoque, Le Moustier. To anyone who, like myself, finds the way in which our knowledge of prehistoric man has been discovered and developed almost as interesting as the modern factual content of prehistoric knowledge, Les Eyzies has this double fascination. Not only do we have here the rock-shelters and caves which illustrate the life and times of Palaeolithic man, but the sites which enabled archaeologists to grope their way towards their knowledge of those times. The rock-shelters and sites around Les Eyzies for me tell not only their story of early man, but the story of the struggle of early archaeology. Whichever way we look at them, these are famous places; as Elisée Reclus has written: 'Les noms des Eyzies, de Laugerie-Haute, de Laugerie-Basse, de la Madeleine, de Tayac . . . ont acquis dans la science un nom impérissable.'

We need not concern ourselves with the niceties of Palaeolithic classification, but there are many names that will be constantly referred to. The earliest classification of the Palaeolithic had distinguished a Lower Palaeolithic, consisting, as we have said, of the Abbevillian (or Chellean) and the Acheulian; a Middle Palaeolithic, consisting of the Mousterian; and an Upper Palaeolithic, which was at first divided into two: the Solutrean, named after Solutré near Mâcon, and the Magdalenian, named after La Madeleine and comprising the material from the rock-shelters of Laugerie Haute, Laugerie Basse and La Madeleine itself, the type site. An Aurignacian had been thought of by Lartet but was left out of the first standard classifications. The Abbé Breuil was responsible for reintroducing this, and in the classification of the Upper Palaeolithic which was met commonly in textbooks of twenty to twenty-five years ago the Upper Palaeolithic consists of three stages, or cultures: first the Aurignacian, then the Solutrean, and, thirdly, the Magdalenian. The Aurignacian was divided by Breuil into three stages, the Solutrean into three, and the Magdalenian into six. More recently the Aurignacian (old style) has been split up into three main stages of cultures—namely, the Chatelperronian, the Aurignacian and the Périgordian (sometimes known as the Gravettian). These are the names used in the most recent works on Palaeolithic prehistory and used in the Abbé Breuil's *Four Hundred Centuries of Cave Art*, which must be for many years the main guide to this subject. When we do use these detailed names we shall here follow this classification, which is set out graphically in the diagram below (Fig. 2).

When the Abbé Breuil in 1952 called his book *Four Hundred Centuries of Cave Art*, there were many raised eyebrows. Was it really possible and sensible to suggest that this art began 40,000 years ago? Since then there have been obtained many

MAGDALENIAN			
SOLUTREAN			
Upper Aurignacian	Perigordian III-IV	Gravettian	Perigordian
Middle Aurignacian	Aurignacian	Aurignacian	Aurignacian
Lower Aurignacian	Perigordian I-II	Chatel-Perronian	Chatel-Perronian

Fig. 2. The divisions of the Upper Palaeolithic. The old Aurignacian has now been renamed in different ways, and the different usages are set side by side for purposes of comparison

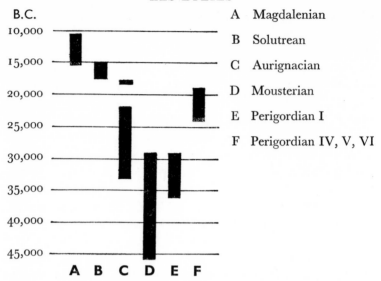

B.C.

A	Magdalenian
B	Solutrean
C	Aurignacian
D	Mousterian
E	Perigordian I
F	Perigordian IV, V, VI

Fig. 3.   *Radiocarbon datings for the Upper Palaeolithic (after Movius)*

radio-carbon dates for the Upper Palaeolithic and these are summarized in the table (Fig. 3) based on the researches of Professor Movius. From this table we see that the Upper Palaeolithic existed from 45,000 B.C. to 10,000 B.C. The earliest Upper Palaeolithic culture with art is the Aurignacian, so that from this table it looks as if Palaeolithic art existed from 35,000 to 10,000 B.C.—so 'four hundred centuries' was not a wrong or misleading phrase. It should be emphasized that these dates are dates of cultural material and not direct dates of the art. We have a few direct dates such as the Middle Magdalenian at Angles-sur-L'Anglin of 12,000 B.C. (in general terms,) and the Magdalenian III deposits at Altamira as 14,000 to 12,500 B.C. A date for Lascaux is often mentioned; it is the date of charcoal associated with rough limestone lamps found near the famous scene and the date was 14,500 to 12,500 B.C. This sample does not date the paintings of course, but if it did Breuil found it unacceptable. He believed the Lascaux paintings belonged to the Aurignacian-Périgordian cycle and must be 35,000 to 25,000 B.C.

The truth is that we do not have enough direct C14 dates for the art as yet, and it may well be difficult to get them. But the chronology based on the cultural materials suggests that the art did last a very long time—at least 25,000 years—and this makes Upper Palaeolithic art one of the really extra-ordinary phenomena in the history of man's art. It is not only the oldest art of man, but the style that lasted the longest.

But we must return from the generalities of Palaeolithic classification to Les Eyzies itself. Before the last phase of the Ice Age, occupation by man was restricted to the plateau itself and the alluvial terraces overlooking the river. Then, as the cold conditions of the Ice Age came on, man moved to occupy the rock-shelters or *abris*, particularly those on the sunny side of the valley sheltered by the steep north hills. During the long, cold, dry period following the close of the Ice Age there flourished the Upper Palaeolithic cultures, with Cro-Magnon man and the remarkable art which will concern us in the next two chapters. It is, of course, possible that Upper Palaeolithic man lived in these rock-shelters only in the winter months, and in the summer roamed widely over France and western Europe. The gradual improvement of climate in post-glacial times changed the steppe and tundra vegetation; the fauna on which Upper Palaeolithic man lived disappeared, and with it the richness of the culture of the Périgord Noir in early times.

This is not to say the area was unoccupied. Neolithic, Bronze Age and Gallo-Roman remains have been found. Here, as in France in general, settlements in Gallo-Roman and later times were mainly located in the valleys. A few of the *abris* have been occupied right down to the Christian era; the majority, how-ever, were abandoned at the end of the Palaeolithic. Medieval settlements, particularly the châteaux and the *maisons-fortes*, took advantage of the cliffs and *abris*. Some were built on tops of the cliffs, commanding a splendid view and being themselves well protected. Others were built in the *abris* halfway up the cliffs, and nearby one can still see holes in the cliffs which served as rooms and lookout posts.

The modern economy of the Périgord Noir is essentially agricultural. Wheat, maize, tobacco, walnuts, vines and fruit trees are grown. There is still some food-gathering though: truffles are collected from the oaks on the limestone plateau in November, with the aid of truffle pigs and truffle hounds. The main cash crops are tobacco, truffles and timber. There are plenty of cattle about, and they are the main animals for draught, milk and meat. The wine trade has declined since the phylloxera in the 'eighties and the great development of the Bordeaux wine area. The traveller walking about from Les Eyzies will constantly come across deserted vine terraces, as well as derelict buildings. There has, in fact, been a considerable decline in the population of the Périgord Noir recently. For example, the population of the commune of Les Eyzies itself has declined by 1,000 since 1890.[1]

Les Eyzies is a curious name; it has been suggested as coming from the Celtic word, *alesia*. The full name of the commune is Les Eyzies-de-Tayac. Tayac now lies about a quarter of a mile from the main village, and is one of the first things to see on visiting Les Eyzies. It consists of an eleventh-twelfth-century fortified church surrounded by a group of scattered houses and farms, many of them derelict. Yet it is perhaps still the ancient religious and socio-cultural focus of the commune. Walking back to my hotel on St John's Day one midsummer, I saw a great glow in the sky behind Tayac Church. We hurried along, and then I realized: here was a St John's, or midsummer, fire. This fine pagan rite was being celebrated on a plot of rough ground not far from the church. A big bonfire of thorn bushes and twigs was burning, and as the flames leapt up, many young men, and one or two of the most fearless young women, jumped through the flames. I was told that, until recently, one would have seen many midsummer fires from Les Eyzies, but now only the Tayac one survives.

From Tayac we can retrace our steps to the village of Les

---

[1] For a general readable account of the human geography of the Périgord Noir see (edited) R. E. Dickinson, *Les Eyzies and District* (Le Play Society, 1934).

Eyzies itself, which is built along the cliffs on the north side of the valley (Plate 4), and at two levels. On the upper *abri* level there was built in the tenth-eleventh centuries a feudal château. The château was restored in the sixteenth century, and one of its most attractive features at the present day is the base of an elegant watch-tower, or sentry-box, of the sixteenth century. Above are the excavations for rooms and lookouts. The main level of the village and the main village street lie on the lower *abri* level, and the newest houses of all are out on the village plain.

Our first job at Les Eyzies, having studied the physical and human geography of the site and seen its various levels of settlement and appreciated the key-points in this settlement pattern —such as the church at Tayac and the château in the centre of Les Eyzies itself—is to observe some of the more celebrated of the *abris* and to visit the Museum. Walking along from Tayac and the railway station, we come first to the *abri* of Cro-Magnon. This is the most obvious site that comes to mind, but, as we have said, it is now occupied by the Hôtel Cro-Magnon, or largely so —the original three famous skeletons were apparently found in what is now the garage—and so there is nothing to see of the original *gisement*. We can make a sentimental pilgrimage to the entrance of the garage and then walk along at the foot of the overhanging cliffs towards the village. Some of the overhanging rocks have been worn by Nature into very strange forms; there is a remarkable mushroom-like affair between the Hôtel Cro-Magnon and the centre of the village. As I walk along this road I always think how warm and sheltered it must have appeared to Upper Palaeolithic man, and how grateful I am that I do not have to live there, with the shadow of the dark, overhanging cliffs always over me. Along these hillsides are rock-shelters and *gisements* which have been dug at various times in the past, and where excavation has proceeded sporadically in recent years. Now a classic and textbook excavation of an *abri* is in progress. This is Abri Pataud, being dug by Professor H. C. Movius of Harvard. These excavations will continue for several years and provide an example of one of the most careful and meticulously recorded excavations one could wish for. Professor Movius will not welcome the publicity these sentences may give to his work. No serious excavator wants to be disturbed constantly by rubber-necks, but he might be persuaded to organize official visits occasionally for those really interested. As you walk along up the main street from the Abri Pataud there is nothing more of interest to see in detail, except to appreciate the exact nature of these *abris*. The most profitable thing is to proceed to the centre of the village and then visit the Museum.

The centre of the village is the Café de la Mairie, where also is housed the Syndicat d'Initiative. Here you can get all the pamphlets and information you want about buses and times of opening of museums and caves and châteaux; here, too, you can sip your *apéritif* or your glass of Monbazillac, or your coffee and liqueur, and watch the lads of the village play *billard-golf* or *footbal* or the electrical and mechanical version of what used to be called Corinthian bagatelle in my youth. Fortified, climb up to the Museum which has been re-planned and re-arranged in recent years. The collections are rich and include the originals of many examples of Upper Palaeolithic art. We should be clear at once that there are, broadly speaking, two kinds of Upper Palaeolithic art; the so-called *art mobilier*, or mobiliary art, which consists of the decorated portable objects, and then the *art parietal*, the parietal (or rock-shelter and cave) art, which is the decoration on the walls of the houses and sanctuaries of Upper Palaeolithic man. Here in the Les Eyzies Museum are some very good examples of the mobiliary art, and it forms a splendid introduction to the great cave art that we are about to see. Also in the Museum is the reconstruction of a Magdalenian burial from St-Germain-la-Rivière in the Gironde: the burial was placed under an odd little construction of stones, almost like a Palaeolithic precursor of a megalithic monument.

The Musée Préhistorique of Les Eyzies was created through the energy of Peyrony, supported by Capitan, Henri Hubert and Paul Léon, then Director of the Beaux-Arts. In 1913 these energetic men acquired for the State the upper terrace at Les

Eyzies, formerly occupied as an Upper Palaeolithic *abri* and later by the medieval and post-medieval château. The first prehistoric collections were installed in a rebuilt and extended château in 1918; the Museum was publicly opened in 1923, and in 1931 Paul Léon unveiled—if that is the right word in this connexion—the statue of a naked primitive man which stands on the edge of the terrace and dominates the view down into the village, as it surprisingly does any view looking up at the château and *abri* from the main road. I do not like this statue, or for that matter any reconstructions of prehistoric men and their life which are violently obtruded on my consciousness as this terrace monster is, but to many, I suppose, it gives a vivid idea of what some prehistoric men may have looked like. I prefer to think of them comfortably decked out in fur coats and capes going efficiently about their business of hunting and of painting and engraving and dancing in their dark caves.

But, whatever you think of the statue, the view from the terrace is splendid. You see before you the whole neighbourhood: the valleys of the Vézère and Beune, away to the left the rounded spur where Font de Gaume is, the little valley leading up to La Mouthe, and on the right, across the river and beyond the railway station, the rocks of Tayac and the overhanging cliffs leading to the Gorge d'Enfer and the Laugeries. Here we can map out, from the terrace of the Museum, our plan of campaign for Les Eyzies. Down the hill—there is no time for any more refreshment at the Café de la Mairie—and across the railway and river to the classic sites between Les Eyzies and the Laugeries.[1]

Crossing the River Vézère and proceeding along the road to Manaurie and Périgueux, you come first to the Roc de Tayac, opposite the village of Tayac. Here the overhanging cliff is 200 to 250 feet high, and there is not much room between cliff and river. A path leads up into these cliffs and takes you to rooms

---

[1] Before leaving the Museum, you should buy Peyrony's *Les Eyzies et les environs: Guide illustré du Savant et du Touriste*, a simple and authoritative guide to the prehistoric sites.

cut in the rock which were used as fortified retreats during the Hundred Years' War. Continuing along the main road, you come to Gorge d'Enfer, a little valley on the left, which has on its left-hand side several interesting sites. The first is famous, and the fame is revealed by its name, which is Grotte du Poisson. It was dug in 1892 and had two occupation levels, one Aurignacian and one Périgordian. In 1912 a Monsieur Marsan discovered, engraved on the roof of this rock-shelter, a salmon (or some comparable fish), and what is described by Peyrony as the head of a bird of prey, but by Breuil as 'according to your fancy . . . the head of an eagle, or a rhinoceros; I prefer the latter interpretation'.[1] This rock-shelter is now inaccessible, so that we cannot go and see the salmon or test our fancy out on rhinoceros and eagle. Its great interest is a personal one, and that is why I have included a photograph of the salmon in the illustrations to this book (Plate 5). Secretly, the then Mayor of Manaurie, Monsieur Delprat, sold this Palaeolithic engraving to the Germans, and it was being cut away under the direction of Otto Hauser with the intention of sending it to the Museum at Berlin when the order of the Beaux-Arts and the approach of the 1914–18 War brought these strange doings to an end. The photograph shows the drill-holes and the undercut shelf whereby it was hoped to remove this most interesting example of Upper Palaeolithic art. It is particularly interesting because fish and birds are seldom represented in this art.

Going along the road to Manaurie from Les Eyzies, you come in a short while to the Laugeries and to the Grotte du Grand Roc. As already pointed out, the Grand Roc is not archaeologically interesting, but is full of splendid natural features, such as stalactites and crystallizations. Close to the entrance to the Grotte du Grand Roc is Laugerie Basse; here there is a guide to show you the *gisements*, a little Museum of finds and a terrace for the *dégustation* of Monbazillac. Laugerie Basse has been dug by various archaeologists since the 'sixties of last century, and it was in one of these sites going by the collective name of Laugerie-Basse that Massenat found a Magdalenian

[1] *Four Hundred Centuries of Cave Art* (1952), p. 305.

(a) The 'hut' at La Mouthe

(b) The fish from the Gorge d'Enfer

6. Sculptured horse at Cap Blanc

skull. It was found in part of the great *abri* belonging to one of the modern houses perched precariously against the hillside. The main *abri* was excavated from 1913 onwards and revealed a splendid stratigraphy of the Magdalenian and then the Neolithic and other levels from the Gallo-Roman to the modern period.[1]

Just under a quarter of a mile further on along the road to Manaurie is Laugerie-Haute. This very famous rock-shelter was discovered by Lartet and Christy in 1862 and first dug by them. It was then dug at various times by people looking for fossils and treasure. It was being excavated by Otto Hauser at the outbreak of war in 1914. Hauser was the man engaged in the negotiations for the removal to Berlin of the Gorge d'Enfer salmon. He was convicted of espionage against the French Government, and in 1921 the State acquired the site. From then on it was excavated by Denis and Elie Peyrony; their excavations were completed in 1935 and a full account of them published three years later. These painstaking and detailed excavations revealed a great sequence of industries, Aurignacian, Périgordian, Solutrean and Magdalenian, and the sections have been neatly left with explanatory boards. Laugerie-Haute is a very large shelter—it is nearly 600 feet in length by 130 feet broad. The excavations were carried down to the bed-rock at a depth varying from 13 to 15 feet. During the excavations at Laugerie-Haute and at Laugerie-Basse engraved or sculptured slabs have been found. In later excavations at the extreme east of Laugerie-Haute Monsieur Maury discovered in 1938 a small Neolithic burial chamber rather like the one reconstructed in the Les Eyzies Museum, and containing several human skulls. These can be seen by enquiring in one of the neighbouring houses.

Our walk through the village of Les Eyzies and along the banks of the Vézère to Gorge d'Enfer and the Laugeries should by now have given us a very clear view of the sort of dwelling-sites of Upper Palaeolithic man. It is time now that we left

---

[1] You can buy at Laugerie-Basse J. Maury's little guide entitled *Sur la Préhistoire et sa Capitale Les Eyzies*.

Museum and rock-shelter and turned to the caves where drawings and engravings were made. After all it is the cave art of the Dordogne that has really brought us to this delectable part of France.

✤ IV ✤

La Mouthe, Font de Gaume
and Les Combarelles

There are four major decorated Upper Palaeolithic caves
to be visited in the Dordogne: La Mouthe, Font de
Gaume, Les Combarelles and Lascaux, and they should
be visited in that order. As we have said before, Lascaux, which
is the best-preserved, should certainly be visited last, and in my
opinion La Mouthe should be visited first, because it is historically interesting and because it produced itself some of the
proofs of the authenticity of this most ancient art.

La Mouthe is just under two miles from the village of Les
Eyzies. You take the road to Campagne and Le Bugue and then
very soon turn off to the left, climbing up a well-signposted
road to the hamlet of La Mouthe—a small collection of farms
and houses, some deserted. A guide will conduct you down to
the site itself, which is about 350 yards from the hamlet. Unlike
Lascaux, La Mouthe has not been equipped with electricity,
and the smell of acetylene lamps will pursue you into the depths
of the hillside.

The opening of the cave faces south across a little valley.
When first known, it looked like a small rock-shelter filled with
occupation debris. In 1895 the proprietor, a Monsieur Lapeyre,
was widening the rock-shelter to serve as a storage-place for
his farm, and while this was going on large numbers of Palaeolithic tools were found, ranging from the Tayacian or Mousterian to the Upper Palaeolithic. By chance, as this was being
done, a gallery was discovered. On 11 April, 1895, four lads set

out boldly to explore this gallery. They were armed with sticks and candles. One of the boys had read about the possibilities of Palaeolithic art; his name was Gaston Bertoumeyrou, and it was he who recognized, well down the gallery, the engraving of a bison. He immediately informed the archaeologist Emile Rivière. Rivière began work at La Mouthe at once and cleared the gallery of the clay which nearly filled it. In September, 1896, he presented an account of the engravings and paintings he had discovered to the Académie des Sciences in Paris, but the learned world was still not ready to accept Palaeolithic art in its entirety.

The story of the discovery of Palaeolithic art has often been told, but we must re-tell its essentials to understand the importance of La Mouthe. In the eighteen-thirties there had been found in the cave of Chaffaud near Sévigné, in the Vienne, a reindeer bone decorated with an engraving of two deer. It is reproduced here (Fig. 4) because it is historically such an interesting piece. It was at first described as Celtic in style, but

Fig. 4. The Chaffaud Deer

when Lartet began working in the Pyrenean and Dordogne caves he found similar works of art, and was able to show that these Upper Palaeolithic hunters were also artists. If you once accepted the antiquity of man and the evidence of the accumulated deposits in the rock-shelters, you had to accept as well the decorated objects that occurred as an integral part of these occupation debris. But this mobiliary art was one thing, the cave art was quite another, and it was the authenticity of the cave art that was hotly disputed, and led to controversies which were settled only at La Mouthe.

The first discovery of cave art was made in the 'seventies of last century. Marcelino de Sautuola began excavating at Altamira in the Cantabrian Mountains, 30 kilometres west of Santander, a few years after 1868, when the entrance to the cave, hidden by a fall of rock thousands of years ago, was discovered quite by chance by a hunter. De Sautuola went on excavating in the cave for years, and found some monochrome paintings in 1875. Four years later his five-year-old daughter Maria was playing in the cave while her father was digging, and she penetrated into a part of it which only a small child could enter standing upright. By the light of her candle she saw a painted animal over her head, and then several more, and ran out to her father saying, '*Toros! Toros!*'—Come and look at the bulls. Her father examined her discovery, and it was in this way there were found the wonderful polychrome paintings of bison and boar and other animals which have made Altamira, with Lascaux, the most famous sites of Upper Palaeolithic art.[1]

De Sautuola realized the importance of his find, and at once attributed the art to the Upper Palaeolithic. He published an account of his discoveries in 1880, but the scientific world was sceptical. Some declared that the paintings had been done by Roman soldiers, and a madman came forward to confess that he had himself done the paintings at de Sautuola's request! This very great discovery, disbelieved in, was forgotten. And, as the Abbé Breuil has himself pointed out, in 1880 the International Congress of Prehistoric Archaeology and Anthropology at Lisbon did not even mention the name of Altamira. Altamira, buried for so many thousands of years by fallen rock, was rediscovered, only to be buried again in oblivion and scepticism.

This is why La Mouthe is so important, as Emile Rivière himself realized. The engravings at La Mouthe had been discovered only *after* the deposits of human occupation had been cleared away. The entrance to the gallery was completely blocked by the undisturbed occupation debris. *Ergo*, these

[1] The story of Sautuola's daughter is the standard archaeological textbook anecdote. In a letter to me dated 9 January, 1953, the Abbé Breuil, who knew Sautuola's daughter when she was grown up, says that she has no recollection of this event, but, the Abbé adds, she was probably too young to remember!

engravings must be older than, or as old as, the Palaeolithic occupation of the cave-shelter. That is what Rivière maintained in his publication to the Académie des Sciences in 1896. Some archaeologists and geologists then came to visit La Mouthe and were convinced by the evidence. They went away convinced of the authenticity of the decorations and of Upper Palaeolithic cave art.

Meanwhile, another site, the cave of Pair-non-Pair, comes into the news. Pair-non-Pair is on the right bank of the River Dordogne just before it joins the Garonne at the Bec d'Ambez and both flow into the sea as the Gironde. It is in the department of the Gironde some sixty miles west of Les Eyzies. François Daleau began to excavate here in 1874. The cave was filled with deposits, and it was only as these occupation deposits were removed that in 1883 Daleau saw some engraved lines on the wall of the cave. He did not think much of them, but in 1896, having heard of the discoveries at La Mouthe, he brought a pump from his vineyard and washed down the walls with a strong spray. In August, 1896, he was able to distinguish an engraved horse, and in November of that year he described to the Archaeological Society at Bordeaux the engravings of twelve animals that he had found. The Abbé Breuil visited Pair-non-Pair in 1898 and 1899, and saw clearly that Daleau had a series of archaeological levels starting with a Mousterian of Acheulian tradition, then a typical Mousterian, succeeded by Aurignacian, Périgordian and Magdalenian. The walls with their engravings were buried under the Périgordian levels and were above the Aurignacian levels. Therefore the engravings must belong to the end of the Aurignacian and to the Périgordian. Here was not merely proof of the authenticity of Upper Palaeolithic art, but proof of the actual period in the Upper Palaeolithic to which it belonged.

To return to the Dordogne proper—to the Les Eyzies district. In October, 1900, the Abbé Breuil was invited by Emile Rivière to visit La Mouthe. He did so and traced the engravings. He realized that they were stylistically identical with Pair-non-Pair; he saw too that the evidence of La Mouthe precluded any view other than that the engravings were Upper Palaeolithic. The Abbé Breuil's tracings were published in the *Revue Scientifique* for 1901. That very year was to see even more remarkable discoveries. A man called Berniche, who had worked for Rivière at La Mouthe and knew the site and the engravings well, declared that he had seen elsewhere in a *grotte* engravings like those of La Mouthe. On 8 September, 1901, his son-in-law, Pomarel, guided Dr Capitan, Denis Peyrony and the Abbé Breuil to what is now the celebrated cavern of Les Combarelles. The entrance was then being used as a stable for oxen. By the light of a single small candle, Pomarel and the three archaeologists penetrated into the hillside and discovered the Palaeolithic engravings.

A week later, on 15 September, Peyrony discovered the paintings in the cavern of Font de Gaume, less than a mile from Les Combarelles, and Capitan and Breuil were at once summoned to see them. The critics, however, were no kinder to the discoveries of Font de Gaume and Combarelles when they were announced than they had been to the discoveries at Altamira, La Mouthe and Pair-non-Pair. At the Congress of the Association Française pour l'avancement des sciences, held in Montauban in 1902, the discoveries were discussed and mainly disbelieved in. But at last a field excursion was organized to Les Eyzies.

The savants on the excursion first visited Font de Gaume and Combarelles. The very great number of the paintings and engravings impressed every one of them, and most of all the fact that some of the paintings and engravings were covered with very ancient concretions. The party then went on to La Mouthe and were convinced by the evidence there—the evidence that the gallery had been discovered only after undisturbed deposits had been cut through, and the fact too that here again some of the engraved lines disappear under stalagmitic concretions.

In his *Four Hundred Centuries of Cave Art* (p. 292), the Abbé Breuil published a photograph of the excursion of the A.F.A.S. to La Mouthe on 12 August, 1902. The photograph shows

Rivière, Peyrony, Emile Cartailhac, Adrien de Mortillet, François Daleau and the Abbé Breuil himself—then only twenty-five years old. It is, as he claims, 'a really historical document, for it dates the day when the scientific world officially recognized the wall art in the caves of the Reindeer Age'. Emile Cartailhac, Professor at Toulouse and then doyen of prehistoric archaeology in France, had disbelieved in Altamira without going to see it. Yet he recognized that Font de Gaume was stylistically the same as Altamira; and in *L'Anthropologie* for 1902 he published, under the title of 'Mea culpa d'un sceptique', a recantation of his views. He said he was mistaken in his dating, and immediately asked the young Breuil to accompany him to Spain and see the site of Altamira, which they then visited together.

Thus it was that La Mouthe played such an important and historic role in the discovery of Palaeolithic art. We should visit the site at present with these facts very clearly in our minds. You first enter the rock-shelter: it is large and low, and the gallery is seen opening away on the left. About 100 metres from the entrance you come to the first figures: engravings of a horse and four oxen—they are vigorously engraved with deep, wide lines. Further on, and immediately after the slight widening of the gallery, the left wall is covered with figures, including bison, stag and ibex. One of the bison on this wall was the figure first recognized by Gaston Bertoumeyrou when he and the other lads entered the gallery in 1895. Further figures of reindeer and rhinoceros are to be found as you proceed along the gallery. Right at the end is a hall about 12 to 14 feet by 9 to 10 feet. The wall on the right is covered with engraved designs, including ibex, reindeer, rhinoceros and mammoth. One of the most curious designs is that of a hut, both engraved and painted. It is in bands of black, red-brown and red separated from each other by carefully scraped zones. From the first time he saw it Emile Rivière described it as a hut. Such representations are rare in Upper Palaeolithic art. A photograph of it is reproduced here (Plate 5).

The next classic site to visit after La Mouthe is Font de

Fig. 5. Mammoth from Les Combarelles

Gaume itself. This is one of what Breuil has called 'The Six Giants' of Palaeolithic Cave Art sites: the others are Combarelles, Lascaux, Altamira, Les Trois Frères and Niaux.[1] Font de Gaume is the site discovered in 1901 by Peyrony. Its entrance is in the valley of the Beune, just over a mile from Les Eyzies. The road out of the village is signposted to Sarlat, and a well-signposted track to the right leads up to the cave entrance. The guide who lives at the little house on the roadside walks up with you unless he is already in session in the cave. The cave entrance is about 70 feet up the cliff-side, and a narrow winding path leads up to it. From the entrance you look back over Les Eyzies. The entrance porch has two galleries leading off: that on the left goes only about 50 feet into the hill; that on the right penetrates the hill for nearly 140 yards and has two short branches leading off it. The width of this long, narrow cave varies from round about 4 to 7 feet. There is one extremely narrow part of it (now reached by an iron ladder)

[1] The first three of the 'Giants' are in the Dordogne, Altamira is in North Spain. Les Trois Frères and Niaux are in the department of the Ariège in the French Pyrenees. See the map of Franco-Cantabrian art, Map 3, (p. 107).

which is called the 'Rubicon', and leads to the inner part of the cave with the painted figures. There are many of these, and the animals portrayed include bison, horse, reindeer, mammoth, oxen, ibex and bear. Some of these are fine polychromes; others monochromes in shaded black. The Abbé Breuil has worked out here and at other sites the succession of styles in Upper Palaeolithic cave art,[1] and here at Font de Gaume most of the styles are represented from the first or Aurignacian-Périgordian cycle and from the second or Magdalenian cycle.

Fig. 6. Cave Bears

The finest paintings from Font de Gaume are the woolly rhinoceros, a red line drawing, the horse, the ox in shaded black, and the splendid pair of reindeer. These reindeer are faded in part and are difficult to see clearly except where specially lit. They appear to be a male and female, the male affectionately snuffling the head of the female. The great joy of Font de Gaume lies in the large paintings of bison and mammoth. There are two other things which the new archaeological

[1] For an account of these styles see Breuil, *Four Hundred Centuries of Cave Art*, especially pp. 37ff. Font de Gaume is described on pp. 75ff.; and there is a whole book on this site: Capitan, Breuil and Peyrony, *La caverne de Font de Gaume aux Eyzies* (Monaco, 1910).

tourist to the Dordogne will observe for the first time here at Font de Gaume, and these are symbols of hands and the so-called 'tectiforms'. Representations of human hands, both negative and positive, are often found in Upper Palaeolithic art. So are the curious symbols called for convenience 'tecti-forms' which may be representations of huts or traps or even symbols of artists or tribes; their precise significance is a matter of guess-work.

Font de Gaume is a fine introduction to Upper Palaeolithic art because of the variety of animals represented and the vigour and naturalness and joy with which some of them are painted. Already one can perceive the special character of Upper Palaeolithic art; it is mainly a naturalistic animal art—it has very few representations of human beings, and it is mainly concerned with the drawing of single animals in side view. There are very few scenes and also no backgrounds.

Les Combarelles is farther along the road to Sarlat from Les Eyzies, and much nearer the road than is Font de Gaume. The guide lives in a cottage close to the site, and as he takes you round he will tell you with pride that the site was discovered by his uncle and his grandfather—the young man Pomarel and his father-in-law, Berniche, whom we have already mentioned. I remember the guide telling me of the excitement these two men had experienced when they discovered these engravings. They had known of the tunnel-like cavern at Les Combarelles for a long while, but it seemed to end in a mass of stalactite and stalagmite. They had observed the amount of this calcitic material, however, that had to be cleared away at La Mouthe, and decided to break away the material at the end of the tun-nel at Les Combarelles in the hope—the remote hope as it then seemed to them—of being able to get through it to a further cave. But their hopes were justified, and they got through the curtain of calcite and walked on into the rest of the tunnel-like cave which no one had visited for thousands of years. The guide will show you with justifiable pride the engravings which they first found.

At present there are two galleries at Les Combarelles, both

opening out of a wide rock-shelter. The main site opening on the left is Combarelles I: this is the one where the engravings were found in 1901. The other site, Combarelles II, was known in Emile Rivière's time: he found Magdalenian tools there. Recently engravings have been found on the walls of this gallery also.

Combarelles I, the main site, which was fully published in 1924,[1] has no side branches and goes on into the hillside for 250 yards. The height varies from 12 feet at the entrance to 5 to 6 feet, or even less, at times. It is always, of course, cold in the depths of the hill. All these walks into the Dordogne limestone hillsides seem much longer at the time than they really are, and longer still in retrospect because of the darkness, the slow progression and the constant bending down to avoid knobs of stalactite or to look at a painting or engraving. Even with the most perfunctory examination of the art at Font de Gaume and Les Combarelles, you must allow at least half an hour for each cave.

Font de Gaume was notable for its paintings; Combarelles is famous for its engravings. Breuil, Peyrony and Capitan have deciphered and described nearly 300 engraved figures here, and noted about another 100 too poor to be traced or described in detail. The animals represented include horses, bison, bears, reindeer, mammoth, ibex, oxen, stags, lions and wolves; the great majority of these engravings are Magdalenian in date. In addition to this fine gallery of engraved animals are a few 'tectiforms' and nearly forty human or semi-human figures, many of which seem to be masked.

Font de Gaume and Combarelles between them give a splendid impression of the possibilities and range of Upper Palaeolithic art, and show its commonest techniques, painting and engraving. But Upper Palaeolithic man was also a sculptor, and at least one of the most famous sites for Palaeolithic sculpture is not far from Combarelles. After leaving Combarelles, go

---

[1] Breuil, Capitan and Peyrony, *La Caverne des Combarelles* (Paris, 1924). Unfortunately this book and the Capitan, Breuil, Peyrony book on Font de Gaume are now out of print.

along the road to Sarlat and then turn off to the road marked 'Tamnies'. In a very short while you will come to a signpost pointing up the hill to the left saying 'Guide', and a little farther on a notice saying that you have arrived at the Abri de Cap Blanc, and that motorists should *klaxoner* for the *guide* and then wait ten minutes until he arrives. On my last visit a party of Swiss had been klaxoning and waiting in vain for well over

Fig. 7. Ibexes and Horses from Les Combarelles

ten minutes. I climbed up the hill myself to find the guide. The path is well signposted and leads to a little hamlet on the plateau which is itself of very great charm, and with a wonderfully rewarding view across the valley of the Beune to the ruined château of Commarque. The hamlet seemed quite empty in the hot midday sun except for clucking hens scratching in the straw of a large barn and white rabbits munching away inside wirefronted packing-cases. After a while a very old man, with shaking hands, appeared from the shade of a walnut tree. He walked with great difficulty, and I thought it might be hours

77

before we got him down to the *abri*. But no, it was his son who was the guide, and the son was summoned from the fields and took us all down to the rock-shelter, which has a brick wall built to protect the sculptures. They are locked up, and it is quite useless trying to see them without a guide. Cap Blanc is well worth waiting to see.

The rock-shelter is on the slope of the rising ground above the Beune. It was explored in 1909–14 by Dr Lalanne, and it

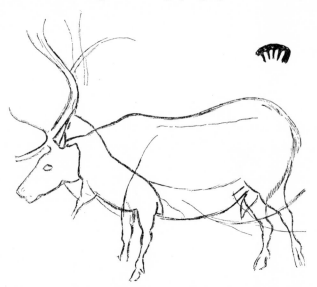

*Fig. 8. Reindeer, Red Deer, and remains of stencilled hand
from Les Combarelles*

was in 1911 that there was found the now world-famous frieze of sculptured animals: a bison, a reindeer or an ox, and several horses. They are carved in high relief, and very cleverly utilize existing irregularities in the rock surface. The excavations in the rock-shelter revealed two hearths of Magdalenian times and a Magdalenian burial, 'perhaps', says Peyrony with pardonable imaginative insight, 'that of the sculptor.' The largest of these magnificent sculptured horses is nearly 7 feet in length from head to tail. When first discovered, it bore traces of red ochre colouring, so that all these sculptures, like so much of our

English medieval and post-medieval stonework, may originally have been brightly painted. One of the Cap Blanc horses is seen in the illustration (Plate 6).

The Cap Blanc discovery was the first discovery of Palaeolithic sculpture. No one had any idea before that there existed Magdalenian sculptures in high relief. Since then other discoveries have been made of sculptures dating from Palaeolithic times in the Dordogne and in the Charente and in Poitou, and we now have to recognize that Palaeolithic man was a modeller as well as a painter and engraver.

The guide who took you to Cap Blanc will also take you to another small rock-shelter nearby, that of La Grèze. Here, in 1904, Monsieur Ampoulange, the excavator, discovered in a small recess the engraved figure of a bison. As with the discovery at Altamira, and for the same reason, it was his small child who made the discovery. The engraving shows very clearly two rather stiffly executed legs in pure profile, but the two horns in twisted perspective.

Two sites in the immediate neighbourhood do not repay a visit. These are Commarque and Laussel. There is no point in visiting them because the rock-shelters are filled in at the present day and the engravings cannot be seen. Laussel is a most famous site and deserves special mention. Here Dr Lalanne found occupation levels from Mousterian to Solutrean. Around the walls on movable slabs were human or animal figures, and on the rock face itself a remarkable engraving always known familiarly to archaeologists as 'the Venus of Laussel'. Dr Lalanne had this figure cut off the rock. All the figures were in his private collection, although one was stolen and sold to Berlin.

The Venus of Laussel is reproduced here (Plate 7). She is one of the *chefs d'œuvre* of Palaeolithic art, and is about 1 foot 8 inches high, originally painted red. She is naked, and shown with great, projecting hips. In one hand she holds what may be a bison's horn. The face is not delineated, and the line of the back of the head running down to the shoulder is surely meant to represent hair. This figure and the others on the movable slabs were grouped together in a portion of the Laussel shelter. It is very difficult, I think, to resist the conclusion that this was some sort of prehistoric shrine and that the Venus of Laussel, like the little sculptures in the round that have been found in Palaeolithic contexts, are some versions of fertility goddesses. However, as always in prehistoric archaeology, the observable facts are easier to record than are the underlying facts to infer. We must, in any case, defer any comment on the nature of the art we have been looking at until we have seen Lascaux, one of the best-preserved examples of this art in France.

Venus of Laussel

8. (*a*) Lascaux: horse in the left, or axial, gallery

8. (*b*) Lascaux: frieze of little horses in left gallery

(a) Lascaux: the 'scene'

(b) Lascaux: the 'scene'

10. (*a*) Rouffignac: the rhinoceros frieze, from Pierret's *Le Périgord Souterrain* (1953)

10. (*b*) Rouffignac: the rhinoceros frieze, photographed after the 'discovery' in June, 1956

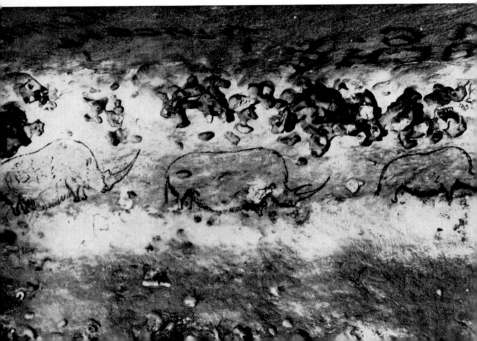

⚜ V ⚜

Lascaux

The road from Les Eyzies to Montignac—the road that is, that leads to Lascaux—leaves from the south end of the village. It climbs over the hill dividing the valley of the Beune from that of the Vézère and then drops down to the Vézère at Tursac, and follows that river valley up the seven or eight miles to Montignac. As you go along this road you pass sites of great interest to the prehistorian. First there is La Madeleine, dug by Lartet and Christy, which gave its name to the classic division of the Upper Palaeolithic, the Magdalenian. It is on the north bank of the river and is difficult of access. Further along the north bank is Le Moustier, a charming little village built at the bottom of the hillside in which is to be found the celebrated rock-shelter which gave its name to the Mousterian. This rock-shelter is very easy of access, and should certainly be visited. It, too, was first excavated by Lartet and Christy. Below it, nearer to the roadway, is a second rock-shelter, partly occupied at present by buildings and partly by the prehistoric *gisement*. This second rock-shelter was first excavated by Hauser in 1907–8, and in the latter year he discovered a Mousterian skeleton which he sold to the Berlin Museum. Later on the excavations were continued by Peyrony, who was able to demonstrate a succession of culture levels where Hauser had found only one.

Not far from Le Moustier is the rock-shelter of Le Ruth. It yielded a succession of overlying deposits excavated by Robert Pages under the direction of Peyrony. The bottom layer was Aurignacian, the next Perigordian, the next three layers were

Solutrean and the top layer was Magdalenian. There was uncertainty at first as to the relationship of the Aurignacian and the Solutrean. In 1908 Peyrony summoned a conference to this small rock-shelter, and it was decided on the spot that the Aurignacian was pre-Solutrean. So Le Ruth, like Le Moustier and La Madeleine, has its place in the history of archaeology —particularly the history of Palaeolithic studies. At present it is a grass-grown sleepy shelter rising out of a small hamlet which, in the somnolent summer afternoon, seems itself fast asleep.

The quiet country town of Montignac which we come to last, exercising strong will power and the good sense that sees the Les Eyzies sites first, is engaged in the manufacture of wood, leather and gut strings for violins and surgical purposes. Until 1940 it had no particular claims to fame, and was content to call itself Montignac-sur-Vézère: since the discovery of the marvellous cave of Lascaux in September, 1940, there has been a pardonable tendency for reasons of publicity to call the village Montignac-Lascaux.

The story of the discovery of Lascaux has often been told; indeed, like the '*Toros! Toros!*' story about Altamira, it is now one of the standard anecdotes of prehistory. Nevertheless, because it is true and relevant and exciting, it demands re-telling. On the morning of 12 September 1940, when the Battle of Britain was being fought out and France itself was divided into an occupied and a so-called unoccupied zone by a line that ran from Bordeaux north-east to Burgundy, five young men from Montignac went out rabbit-shooting. They were Ravidat, Marsal, Queroy, Coencas and Estreguil. Ravidat, Marsal and Queroy were local boys; the other two were refugees from occupied France. Ravidat, aged seventeen at the time, was the oldest of the five and the leader of the party. They had with them two guns and a dog—a famous dog to whom archaeologists should erect a statue—the little dog Robot.

The boys climbed about on the ridge of hill called Lascaux, which belonged, and still belongs, to the Comtesse de la Rochefoucauld, and which lies to the south of Montignac. Twenty years before their expedition a storm had blown down a tall fir tree, and the hole revealed by its torn roots did not fill in. A donkey fell in, broke his legs and died. On 12 September 1940 the dog Robot disappeared down this hole. The young lads had no idea what had happened to him and shouted his name. Muffled barks came from within the hillside, and at last they stood around the tree-root hole where the donkey's bones lay whitening. Ravidat, the dog's owner, decided he would go down the pot-hole and rescue Robot. The five young men widened the hole with sticks and knives until it was large enough for Ravidat to slip through. He slithered down by rope on to the slippery floor of a cave 25 feet below the surface of the earth. The other lads followed him. They lit matches. There was Robot, and in the gloom around them on the walls of the cave were the magnificent paintings of the main hall of Lascaux which now make the small town of Montignac a place of world pilgrimage—horses, stags, bulls. Marsal, Ravidat and the others were the first to see this art for 15,000 years.

When they got back to Montignac, the five lads did not at first tell anyone else. For five days they kept their amazing discovery to themselves, and while they guarded this secret they explored the cave fully. Then they told their old schoolmaster, Léon Laval, who had taught them about Upper Palaeolithic art and taken them to see the famous caves of Font de Gaume and Combarelles. Monsieur Laval thought they were pulling his leg, but changed his mind as soon as he got inside the cave. On 21 September the Abbé Breuil, who was staying at Brive, on the borders of occupied and unoccupied France, twenty miles from Lascaux, came over to see the new discoveries. He studied the paintings and drawings together with other pre-historians. Less than a year later the Abbé Breuil, Monsieur Peyrony and the Comte Begouen held a sort of informal inquest on their discoveries and decided that Lascaux was to be closed to the general public for the time being. In October, 1940, a preliminary report by Breuil was presented to the Académie des Inscriptions et des Belles Lettres in Paris. In this report Breuil said that, if Altamira was to be described as the capital of prehistoric cave art, then Lascaux was the 'Versailles de la Préhistoire'.

After the war the Historical Monuments Commission of the French Government took charge of Lascaux. The *aménagements* are, as always—or almost always—in French antiquities, very well carried out indeed. Two massive doors protect the cave from the outside, and the cave itself is well and tastefully lit. Lascaux is just over a mile from the centre of Montignac, and is open to the public most of the year from 9.30 a.m. to 12 noon and, after a long midday gap, from 2 p.m. to 7 p.m. Two of the guides and guardians are the original discoverers, Ravidat and Marsal, although, alas! the real original discoverer, the little dog Robot, is no longer.

I first saw Lascaux in the spring of 1948 soon after it had been opened to the public, and have seen it almost every year since then. It is one of the prehistoric sites which never palls and which always, on each visit, lives up to one's memory of it. Indeed, it always seems to me that the Lascaux in one's mind's eye is not so brightly coloured and the paintings are not so vigorous and breath-taking as the reality when one sees it again. A visit to Lascaux is not long; unlike Font de Gaume and Combarelles, there is no scrabbling through narrow passages and a long walk before the Palaeolithic art is found. You pass through the second door, and within a minute from leaving the sunshine of the hillside and the postcard stalls you are in the main hall, or, as it is often called, the Hall of Bulls. This is a good name, because one of the main features of this first hall is the fresco of bulls. Four of these bulls are intact, and there are two others not complete—the largest of the bulls is as much as 16 to 17 feet long. They are all painted in black outline, probably with manganese, and the surfaces spotted with black. These fine black bulls are painted on top of older paintings in dark red ochre.

The first animal on the left as you enter the hall, and before you see the bulls, has caused a great deal of comment, and has been nicknamed the Unicorn. Its body is that of a rhinoceros, but its head (according to Miss Dorothea Bate) is that of the

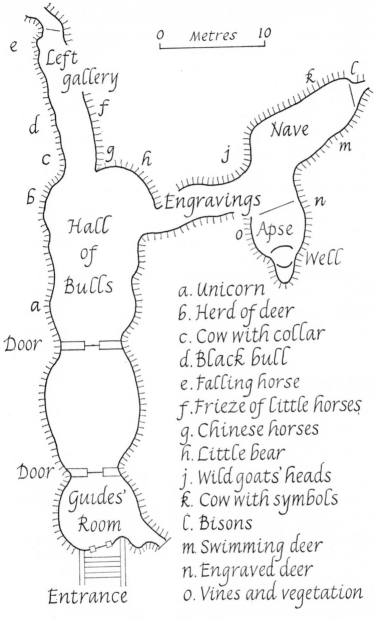

e

Left
gallery

f

d

g h

c

Nave

k l

m

j

b

Engravings

n

Hall

o Apse

of

Well

Bulls

a. Unicorn

a

b. Herd of deer

Door

c. Cow with collar

d. Black bull

e. Falling horse

f. Frieze of little horses

g. Chinese horses

h. Little bear

j. Wild goats' heads

Door

k. Cow with symbols

Guides'

l. Bisons

Room

m. Swimming deer

n. Engraved deer

Entrance

o. Vines and vegetation

0 Metres 10

Fig. 9. Plan of Lascaux

85

pantholops, the Tibetan antelope. From the main Hall of the Bulls a passage leads off to the right, and another goes straight on. For convenience of reference we may call these the right-hand passage, leading to apse and nave, and the left-hand gallery; these are the names by which they are known in the books.[1] The right-hand passage or lateral passage, as it is sometimes called, leads into two wider areas of the cave called the apse and the nave; among the astonishing treasures of Palaeolithic art to be found here are the frieze of stags' heads, and the splendid pair of male bison tail to tail painted in dark brown. On the left-hand wall of the nave below the forelegs of a painted cow are curious polychrome, nine-squared, chequered figures. No one has succeeded in explaining the meaning of these figures, unless they be, like one explanation of the 'tectiforms', marks of artists or tribes.

From the end of the apse there opens up a vertical pit or well, which is not open to the general public. At the bottom is painted one of the most remarkable things in the art of Lascaux, or, for that matter, in Upper Palaeolithic art. This scene is reproduced here (Plate 9) because of the impracticability of visiting it. First of all there is a bison with head down; he has been transfixed with a spear and his innards are tumbling out. In front of the bison is a very oddly drawn man falling backwards. The man has a birdlike head. Nearby is a bird on the end of a rod, and in front a spear-thrower, while further to the left is a rhinoceros. What does all this mean? Has the hunter been himself killed in the act of hunting the bison, and is the bird on a stick his totem? It is all a matter of guesswork. We have already commented on the absence of human beings from Palaeolithic art, and the absence of scenes. That is what makes this Lascaux painting so unusual and interesting.

The left-hand or axial gallery has many wonderful works of

[1] Lascaux has already a considerable literature. A. H. Brodrick produced *Lascaux: A Commentary* in 1949 (London, Lindsay Drummond); F. Windels's *Lascaux* was published in French at Montignac in 1949 and in English under the title of *The Lascaux Cave Paintings* by Faber and Faber, London, in 1949. A. Laming and M. Roussell's pamphlet, *The Cave of Lascaux*, can be bought at the site.

Upper Palaeolithic art; the visitor should note particularly the frieze of little horses over which a cow seems to be jumping (Plate 8, bottom), the horse falling upside down at the end of the gallery, and the roof paintings of cattle and horses. You can visit Lascaux many times and still be surprised by the delightful masterpieces you had forgotten about. The best way to get the most out of Lascaux is to visit it in the morning, having driven over from Les Eyzies. Then, with the paintings and engravings fresh in your mind, climb up the hill to the little farmhouse which now advertises itself as the Café-Restaurant Bellevue. Here you can sit on the terrace looking out over the Vézère Valley, or, best of all, eat lunch. You will be given an inexpensive and exciting lunch—*foie gras, confit d'oie, omelette aux truffes, salade,* and then perhaps *beignets,* with white and red wine—everything, including the wine, but with the exception of the salt and sugar, the product of this charming hill farm.

And while you savour your lunch you can think over the problems which crowd into the average traveller's mind as he sees Lascaux. Is it genuine? We have spoken about the controversy relating to the authenticity of Upper Palaeolithic art that raged from the discoveries at Altamira to the famous day at La Mouthe. By now most people accept Upper Palaeolithic cave art, but when Lascaux was discovered, some said, could it be true? It was and is so much fresher and better than the other sites. That is due to the special circumstances of its position. It is well below the level of the ground and unaffected by frosts and changes of temperature. Many of the paintings, moreover, have been made on a thin calcitic film, which acted as a varnish on the wall and has made the paintings keep their colour more than have those of many other Palaeolithic caves. Yes, Lascaux is a genuine example of Upper Palaeolithic cave art. What, then, do these painted and engraved caves mean?

The entrance by which you now visit Lascaux is not the original entrance. This has yet to be found, and it may well be that, originally, at Lascaux, as at Font de Gaume and Combarelles and La Mouthe, a long passage led in from the open hillside to the dark, painted chambers within the hill. Why were these caves painted with animals? Many explanations have been suggested at various times. These are not houses or tombs. They must be special places of assembly, not, surely, art galleries, but of special assembly for magico-religious purposes. Did you notice at Lascaux that some of the animals have arrows and spears drawn across their sides? (Plate 8, top.) This is quite a common feature of Upper Paleaolithic art, and the most cogent explanation we can give at present is that perhaps sympathetic magic was practised in these dark caves; that around and on the paintings and drawings rites were enacted that guaranteed or were hoped to guarantee the success of the hunter. This is, of course, guesswork, as all explanations of prehistoric art and symbolism must be, but it seems to fit all the puzzling features of this art: its remoteness, the fact that paintings and drawings are often put on top of each other, the concentration of animals —and often of pregnant animals—and the arrows and spears drawn in their sides. These were probably fertility and hunting magics, and in other Palaeolithic sites, though not in these we have been looking at in the Dordogne, there are clearly shown masked human figures. These masked figures—humans wandering around in animal masks—were the priests or medicine men, or artists as well, who controlled and assisted at whatever rites took place in these ritual caves.

But even if we do not agree with this explanation of the purpose of this art, we can admire its vigour and energy and natural charm. We have to wait a great time in the history of European art before we find again the same naturalistic treatment of animals we have here. Indeed, some would say that there is a Walt Disney feel about some of the animals—like the little horses in the axial gallery. Your lunch finished, go down the hill and see Lascaux again, and pause, taking in these fine bulls and horses. You are seeing these paintings under the best possible circumstances of lighting. We know that prehistoric man, who 15,000 to 20,000 years ago explored these caves and made these paintings, had lamps of limestone in which he burnt vegetable oil, but it would be a very different thing painting these frescoes by such light, and a very different thing from our present viewing when the great hall of the bulls was full of masked figures lit up by these guttering lamps and by torches. It may well be that we are in the present century the first persons to see Upper Palaeolithic art well lit as art, and not poorly lit as magico-religious symbolism.

There are two final reflections as you walk down or drive down in your car to Montignac. Are the paintings in Lascaux fading, due to their present exposure to light and their inspection every day by hundreds of visitors? At least this is the question you could have asked yourself up to 1962; now we know the answer—the paintings are fading. There has been for years a great dispute about all this, some saying that the paintings were fading, and others that the apparent fading was a subjective memory of a first visit when the great paintings appeared more marvellous and clearer than on subsequent visits. I was assured a few years ago by Monsieur Severin Blanc of Les Eyzies, then Director of Antiquities in the Dordogne, that the alleged fading was a legend, and that no change in the appearance and quality of these paintings had taken place since that remarkable day in September, 1940, when the five boys dropped into the hillside and discovered this prehistoric temple. In October, 1954 the Abbé Breuil assured me that there was no deterioration in the Lascaux paintings as far as he could judge during the fifteen years that he had been studying them. But these views were expressed to me eight years ago and even then others were taking a more gloomy view. In the last eight years the view that something was wrong has been gaining ground, and recently a most distinguished and knowledgeable archaeologist wrote to me, 'For some years now, it has been quite obvious to those of us who have been in the habit of visiting Lascaux at fairly frequent intervals, that the colour (particularly the red) has been fading.' It was hoped that the air-conditioning would solve everything. What it certainly did do was remove the complaints of visitors in pre-air-conditioning days who said they could not breathe for lack of air.

Now (1963) we know that the colours *are* fading and that a green micro-organism of seaweed structure is growing over some of them—especially the great bull—and that the rock surface is crumbling. The question at the moment, as we go to press, is, can the paintings be saved? Lascaux was closed early in the spring of 1963, and will be closed while experiments are conducted. The French Government has set up a large committee of scientists under Monsieur Henri de Segogne to try and find a way of stopping the fading and eradicating the mysterious algae growth. The humidity of the air, its movement and the chemical content of the atmosphere will be measured, and it is hoped then that it may be possible to decide whether the growth of the algae is being caused by the visitors or by the mechanism installed in 1952 to condition the air and keep it in motion. It may well be that Severin Blanc and the Abbé Breuil were right and there was no deterioration until the air-conditioning mechanism was installed. If so, the cave may be open to the public again, but a public that may occasionally be short of breath!

However that may be, everyone can rest assured that the French Government through Monsieur André Malraux, the Minister for Cultural Affairs, is taking vigorous steps to deal with the new Lascaux problem. By the time these words are in print and being read in 1964 they may have solved the problem. If not, and if the result of the experiment is that no control is feasible, then it is possible that Lascaux will be closed to the public for all time. But we are assured that before this very extreme measure is taken, every possible other course will be tried. It would indeed be a tragedy if these marvellous paintings were hidden away for all time. I feel sure that the ingenuity and scientific skill of the French will find a way of preserving the paintings and that Lascaux will be back on the list of sites that must be seen in the Dordogne in 1965 (or even earlier).

The first report of the committee published in June 1963 suggested that the deterioration of the paintings at Lascaux was more extensive than was at first suspected. The mould had spread tenfold over the walls in the three previous months and was encroaching dangerously on the paintings.

The second inevitable reflection on leaving Lascaux is this.

LASCAUX

We were all excited by the chance discovery of this remarkable site in 1940; how many more exciting stories such as this one will there be to be told in the next fifty or a hundred years? When the first edition of this book was published I wrote, 'It is only fifteen years since Lascaux was discovered. I cannot believe that the quiet Dordogne hillsides do not contain more such prehistoric sanctuaries. But it may well take more than the accident of a dog falling down a hole to find them.' (*Lascaux and Carnac*, p. 77). That was in 1955. In the following year it was announced that a new discovery of even greater importance than Lascaux had been made in the Grotte de Miremont or Rouffignac. The story of this belongs to the next chapter.

⚜ VI ⚜

Rouffignac

The name Rouffignac was mentioned in this book almost for the first time in the last few words of the previous chapter. It is on the map of sites (p. 39) near Les Eyzies but has not been included in the section on the history of the discovery of Upper Palaeolithic art or in the brief catalogue of sites to be visited. This is because there has been, and still is, controversy about the date and nature of the paintings and engravings in this cave. It should be the last site to be visited by the traveller in search of Palaeolithic art in the Dordogne; he should certainly visit the site—Rouffignac, *la Grotte aux Cents Mammouths*, as the tourist posters describe it—but only after he has seen the major sites near Les Eyzies and formed some impression of the nature of Palaeolithic art.

The village of Rouffignac is about eleven miles north of Les Eyzies and eight miles south-west of Thenon. There are plenty of sign-posts showing the way to the site which is on the estate of La Pradelie. The entrance to the cave is about a mile from the main road. It may be visited from Easter to November, and the tour of the cave is made in open coaches of an electric light railway operated and conducted by Monsieur Plassard who farms La Pradelie and who himself built the railway. The visitor sees no art for the first mile or so then he comes across the famous rhinoceros frieze; this is where the cave splits into two—the branch going north has been christened the Henri Breuil Gallery, the branch going north-west leads to a low flat ceiling—the Grand Plafond. The north or right-hand branch forming the Henri Breuil Gallery has in addition to the rhinoceros frieze between thirty and forty painted and engraved mammoths. The left-hand or north-western gallery contains a large number of engravings and the Grand Plafond is almost entirely covered with large black outline paintings. In the same areas of the cave as the paintings there are a great number of inscriptions—names of people like Dubois and Barry—dating from the eighteenth century onwards. The total number of animals painted and engraved at Rouffignac is more than a hundred and forty; mammoths predominate—there are twenty-seven painted mammoths and forty-three engraved representations; the other animals shown include rhinoceros, ibex, horse and bison.

When the first edition of this book was written in 1955 no-one, at least no-one who wrote in archaeological journals and books, had heard of any Palaeolithic art at Rouffignac, or the Grotte de Miremont as it was most often called then. The discovery of the art at Rouffignac was made by Professor Nougier of the University of Tolouse and Monsieur R. Robert of Tarascon-en-Ariège on 26 June 1956 and announced at the *Congrès Préhistorique de France* in Poitiers on 20 July of that year. Before this the site had been visited by the Abbé Breuil who had no doubts about its authenticity and was tremendously impressed by the importance of the discovery. Other visits culminated in a visit of some thirty archaeologists from various countries on 12 September. I was happy to be invited to join this party which included some distinguished specialists in Palaeolithic art like Professor Martin Almagro of Madrid and Professor Paolo Graziosi of Florence, general prehistorians like myself, and some people who knew the country well like Monsieur Severin Blanc who was then in charge of antiquities in the Les Eyzies area. When this visit was over most of the party signed one of two declarations, the first saying that all was authentic, the second that nothing had been seen to show that Rouffignac was *not* authentic. I myself signed neither declaration and escaped away from the cave as did another non-signatory, Mademoiselle de St-Mathurin, whose knowledge of Upper Palaeolithic art is certainly wider and deeper than that of many who signed the authenticity document. Mademoiselle de St-Mathurin was doubtful of the authenticity of the paintings and has not minced words on this issue from that day to this.

How had this issue of authenticity come about and why were there doubts about paintings authenticated by Breuil, Nougier, Almagro and Graziosi? It began when archaeologists noticed that some of these paintings had been published three years before the 'discovery' in June, 1956. They were published in a little book by Bernard Pierret entitled *Le Périgord Souterrain*, and we include here a copy of this historic photograph (Plate 10) with beneath it a photograph of the same frieze of rhinoceroses being examined by the Abbé Breuil.

Now there are many mysteries about Rouffignac, and the first is why French archaeologists, or at least those living and working in the Périgord, did not, on seeing the Pierret illustration in 1953, immediately visit Rouffignac and make the discovery which Nougier and Robert did three years later. Some people with whom I have discussed this matter do not find it odd, but to me it is very surprising. This little book describing the caves of the Dordogne was available in bookshops in Périgueux, Les Eyzies, Toulouse, Bordeaux, Brantôme—in the places where interested archaeologists and speleologists congregated. Indeed one asks why did not Nougier and Robert themselves make this discovery in 1953 (unless, like myself, they had bought a copy of *Le Périgord Souterrain*, but not cut the pages until 1956!).

But the second mystery to me, when I had cut the pages on hearing of the 1956 discovery and seeing that the rhinoceroses were known about at least three years before, was that there was no mention of them, so clearly shown in the photograph, in the text. Why had not Bernard Pierret, the young author of this book, commented on the frieze of rhinoceroses behind his camp? Because, say Nougier and Robert, 'he saw the paintings . . . but did not understand.' Because, says Pierret himself, he knew them to be of recent date! When Severin Blanc heard of the discovery in June, 1956, he said he knew the rhinoceros frieze well and that 'he examined it at the request of a cave-explorer named Bernard Pierret, who made detailed visits to the Miremont cave every year and was surprised to see these animals appear on a wall they had always seen unpainted. That was in 1949.' But if all this is so, and the rhinoceros frieze was known to Blanc and Pierret to be modern, surely when *Le Périgord Souterrain* was published in 1953, one would have expected the author to have a note saying 'the rhinoceroses above the camp were painted in the late 'forties.' This silence certainly has produced mystery and confusion in the minds of those who like myself are trying to sort out the rights and wrongs of this site.

The visits of Pierret and his colleagues to the cave of Rouffignac were between 1945 and 1949. Pierret says he did not visit the cave after 1949 when it was closed by its owner. The photograph published in 1953 therefore dates from 1949, seven years before its official discovery! It has seemed to many people very surprising that the knowledge of these paintings could have been confined, between 1949 and 1956, to Pierret, his friends, to Monsieur Severin Blanc and a few others.

Certainly the statements of Pierret and Severin Blanc caused surprise and astonishment in 1956, and from that day to this the site has been the centre of controversy. On one issue we need be in no doubt. The cave was well known and visited long before Nougier's discovery in 1956 or Pierret's visits in the 'forties. We have referred to the many dates and names painted on the walls by visitors. Baedeker's *Southern France* (I quote from the fifth edition of 1907) has the following entry under the railway station of Mauzent-Miremont:

About 3 miles to the East of the Station is the Grotto of Miremont or Cro de Granville, the galleries of which measure altogether about 3 miles in length. The 'Grande Branche' is about 1100 yards long and contains remarkable stalactites and stalagmites, fossil shells, etc. The guide whose attendance is necessary, lives close by. The entrance is narrow and the ground almost everywhere slippery; the atmosphere cold and damp. To see the whole would take eight hours, but curiosity may be satisfied in two. The most interesting points bear more or less appropriate names.

What a pity that guide, whose attendance was necessary, is not alive to tell us what he showed people on his tours and whether he pointed out any of those paintings which are now so clear and obvious.

Naturally Nougier and Robert have no doubts about the authenticity of Rouffignac and no one has ever questioned their good faith. They have published and described the paintings and engravings believing them all to be authentic, and were strengthened in their view by the support of Breuil, Graziosi, Almagro and many other distinguished scholars. They published a general account in *Rouffignac ou La Guerre des Mammouths* (Paris, 1957; English edition, 1958) and *Rouffignac: I. Galerie Henri Breuil et Grand Plafond* (Florence, 1959). They cite descriptions of the cave in the sixteenth, seventeenth and eighteenth centuries which refer to altars, mosaics and paintings in the generalized terms of travel books of those periods. They also quote the testimony of Monsieur de Laurière, a native of the Rouffignac district, who owns the Château de La Marzelle at Fleurac, near Rouffignac—indeed a house facing the cave on the far side of the valley. De Laurière said in 1956 that he had twice visited Miremont in the summer of 1938, had seen the paintings but had not drawn attention to them because of the controversies that had raged in the previous ten years about the authenticity of the archaeological finds made at Glozel near Vichy, finds now generally regarded as forming one of the classic archaeological forgeries like Piltdown Man. As far as we know, de Laurière is the only person who has said he saw the Rouffignac paintings before 1945.

In his report on Rouffignac communicated to the Académie des Inscriptions et Belles-Lettres on 7 September 1956 (and printed in English as an appendix to the English edition of the Nougier-Robert book), the Abbé Breuil, while referring to 'the very legitimate doubts of M. Pierret and his fellow cave-explorers', goes over the arguments for the authenticity of the paintings; he emphasizes the presence of names dating from the eighteenth and the first half of the nineteenth century and done with smoke from a lamp, and says that these are *superimposed on the drawings* and at a time when nothing was known of Upper

. Mas d'Azil. Spearthrower of bone carved in the form of a woodcock

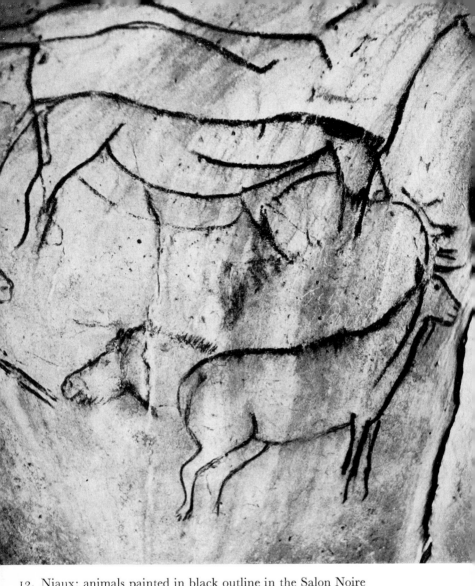

12. Niaux: animals painted in black outline in the Salon Noire

Palaeolithic art. He believed all the paintings and drawings to belong to either a single artist or a group of artists belonging to a single school, and he places them in the beginning of his second cycle of Upper Palaeolithic art either to the last phase of the Gravettian or to the pre-Magdalenian. Almagro declared (11 September 1956): 'I came to examine the whole body of art at Rouffignac in a completely critical spirit. I systematically sought all possible evidence of non-authenticity. I declare in the most unequivocal and categorical manner that I found none. The paintings and drawings at Rouffignac are incontestably authentic and they form one of the finest collections of rock-drawings in the world.' Professor Paolo Graziosi of the University of Florence whose *L'Arte Dell'Antica Età Della Pietra* (Florence, 1957; English edition, London, Faber and Faber, 1960), is one of the most outstanding, complete and reliable works on Palaeolithic art, declared on 9 August 1956, following a visit to Rouffignac: 'Having examined the paintings and drawings discovered hitherto very attentively for many hours, I can affirm most categorically that these paintings and drawings are among the finest and most interesting that the whole series of palaeolithic rock paintings has yielded to us until the present time. I am absolutely astonished that anyone should have started a controversy over the authenticity of these specimens. It is enough to have normal experience of prehistoric art to realize at once, not only their genuineness, but their extraordinary interest. . . . I wish to emphasize the exceptional beauty and delicacy of the drawings on the "Great Ceiling".' These are powerful testimonies which must carry very great weight with all interested in the problem.

Those who are not yet convinced of the authenticity of the Rouffignac paintings are unmoved by the Abbé's arguments that eighteenth and nineteenth century names *overlie* the paintings and do not find this proven. The study of superimpositions of painted lines in caves is a very difficult one, and it *cannot* be proved that these names overlie or underlie the animal paintings. Stylistically some of the paintings seem almost normal Upper Palaeolithic art—the rhinoceroses and mammoths for example—but this style can easily be copied by good artists (and indeed is copied by those decorating the walls of museums, for example, or the reconstructions of Upper Palaeolithic sites, like that at the Château Fort de Reignac); but equally well some of the art, particularly the stiff squarish animals on the Grand Plafond, is unlike most of Upper Palaeolithic art. A distinguished French prehistorian with wide experience of Palaeolithic excavation and art once said to me firmly and quietly, 'I believe there are two styles represented at Rouffignac —one is a pastiche copy of other Palaeolithic art, the other is *Babar l'Eléphant.*'

Those who are not convinced of the authenticity of all the paintings and engravings at Rouffignac draw attention to the curious fact that no one described them in the forty years that elapsed between the discovery of Font de Gaume and Combarelles and the authentication of Palaeolithic art in 1901, and the discovery of Lascaux in 1940. What, they ask, were the archaeologists and speleologists in the Dordogne doing all this time? Surely they were examining every known cave looking for more art like La Mouthe and Font de Gaume. And surely, when Lascaux was discovered, they must have redoubled their efforts to make more discoveries. I look at *l'Affaire Rouffignac* not only as an archaeologist and an archaeologist particularly interested in the history of the creation and revelation of forgery but as a reader (and occasionally writer) of detective stories. I have already said there are to me many strange things about the history of Rouffignac: one is certainly this—why did the keen people working in the Dordogne between 1900 and 1940 not find the paintings at Rouffignac? The answer given by one side of the controversy is a simple one, 'Because they were then not there to find', but a simple answer is not necessarily a true one.

The doubters naturally draw attention to the evidence of Pierret and Severin Blanc, and it is not only the evidence of these men which is before us. Monsieur William Martin, a French schoolmaster despite his English-sounding name, and a keen speleologist, now in the Schools Advisory Service at Périgueux, told me that he too had seen the walls at Rouffignac, now covered with paintings, when they had been bare, and at my suggestion he wrote a letter containing this information to the *Sunday Times* of London where it was published on 1 March 1959. I quote from this letter:

> I assert categorically that in September, 1948, there were no paintings or engravings in the Rouffignac cave. . . . In 1946 together with other young men, I founded the Spéléo Club Périgourdin; our object was to make a complete list of all the caves in the department of the Dordogne, and to find the reason, for example, for a re-appearance of certain subterranean streams. From the beginning Rouffignac attracted our attention . . . our own very numerous explorations enabled us to extend to seven kilometres the extent of the cave. . . . Our first task was to re-draw and check the plan made by Martel in 1898 and the measurements we had to make for this involved every nook and cranny of the cave. In no place at any time did we find traces of any paintings or engravings. One day I personally spent from 7 a.m. to 6 p.m. looking specifically for traces of early art and failed to find anything. The last time I visited Rouffignac was September 1948 and on that occasion I spent three days underground. I can confirm that the frieze of rhinoceroses was not then on the wall of the gallery in which we set up our tents. In December 1949 I learned from M. Bernard Pierret that two rhinoceroses had been painted on the wall, and by Easter a third. Let us then no longer speak of the authenticity of this rhinoceros frieze.

It has been suggested that Pierret and Martin were prejudiced witnesses, cross that they had spent so many hours in the cave and never observed the paintings. But they must have been blind if this was so—the paintings are so clear. And it was not only these local speleologists who had also been apparently blind. In 1915 the Abbé Breuil had himself visited Rouffignac with his friend Alluaud; it was a short visit and they were looking for beetles: they saw no paintings or engravings. In 1948 Dr Koby and the Abbé Glory visited Rouffignac; it was a short visit and they were looking for good marks of cave-bear claws: they saw no paintings, although they found plenty of claw-marks as Breuil and Alluaud found their beetle. In their book, *The Cave of Rouffignac*, Nougier and Robert attempt to laugh off these visits, and those of Pierret and his associates, as due to 'specialization and lack of time', and add 'everyone finds what he seeks at Rouffignac'.

In March-April 1939 the Cambridge University Speleological Society went on a caving expedition to Les Eyzies. One of its members (Colonel Arthur Walmesley-White) sent me this account of the Society's visit to Miremont-Rouffignac. I quote from his letter to me dated 27 September 1956:

> We did go to Miremont one day. I don't recollect why we went as I don't think we expected either desirable caving or any archaeological interest. . . . The owner of the cave was very keen to come with us . . . he had put a palisade and gate across the entrance and he seemed to be much concerned as to how he might in some way commercialize the place. We followed a number of the many branches of the cave and I am fairly certain that we never saw any drawings or paintings and that the owner didn't know of any . . . I do not remember any drawings at all. Certainly we were quite conscious of such things having seen some of the more notable caves around Les Eyzies. . . . I see from my notes that we were at Miremont 31 March, 1939.

Now all this is negative evidence. It adds up perhaps to no more than that many people visited the site before 1948 and saw nothing, but negative evidence is evidence of at least seeing nothing: I would be happier to brush it aside if the paintings were difficult to see or if there were more positive evidence than the testimony of this one man Monsieur de Laurière. Then there is Edouard Martel, the great French speleologist. He made a plan of the cave of Miremont-Rouffignac in 1893, spending three days doing it and being assisted by French military surveyors. He mentions no paintings and Nougier, aware of the damaging effect of Martel's negative evidence, says that Martel must have seen the paintings but kept his silence because of the scepticism aroused by the discovery of Altamira in 1879. But Martel did not die in the 'nineties: he lived through to see Palaeolithic art an accepted thing, and in 1930 wrote a book called *La France Ignorée* in which he describes

La Mouthe, Les Combarelles, Font de Gaume and Altamira. And in this book he says of Rouffignac, 'Bref, tout l'intérêt du Cro de Granville est exclusivement d'ordre géologique.' In a note on this and other literary evidence about Rouffignac Mademoiselle de St-Mathurin said (*Antiquity*, 1959, p. 135), 'Martel, then, did not see the Rouffignac paintings.' I think she is right and here I think it should be said that in my opinion he did not see them because they probably were not there. In the same article we have quoted Mademoiselle de St-Mathurin analyses with care and scholarship the alleged observations of the paintings in the sixteenth and seventeenth centuries, and concludes, 'The attempt to provide historical evidence for the existence of Palaeolithic paintings in this cave is built on sand.'

Now let us take stock of where we are at this moment in the discussion of this vexing and worrying affair. In an editorial in *Antiquity* in 1958 (p. 218) I said, '*L'Affaire Rouffignac*, like all tales of disputed antiquities, has four aspects. There is first—though it ought to be last—the subjective judgement of expert art-historians, archaeologists and artists. Secondly there is the technical evidence. Thirdly there is the history of the site, particularly the gossip of the last twenty years. And lastly there is the treatment of the issue by the protagonists. It is this last issue which comes first in the eyes and mind of a jury in an English court—the demeanour and character of defendants and witnesses.' And I added, 'If any book could do harm to the defence it is *Rouffignac ou La Guerre des Mammouths*.' (This is the book originally published in Paris in 1957 and re-issued—with some interesting omissions—in English in 1958 as *The Cave of Rouffignac* to which we have already referred.)

As Editor of *Antiquity* I got Miss Dorothy Garrod to review this book. She seemed to me the person who, with the widest knowledge of comparative archaeology and an intimate knowledge of Palaeolithic art combined with a scrupulous fairness and an integrity rarely equalled in any other prehistorian, should review this for us and tell the world how to resolve the strange affair. Her review was published in the December 1958 number of *Antiquity* and should be read by everyone interested in this fascinating problem. She refers to Denis Peyrony who was the discoverer of Font de Gaume and Combarelles (and Severin Blanc's predecessor at Les Eyzies), and says of him that he 'was always on the lookout for new cave paintings' and 'told his son that there was nothing at Miremont' but, in all fairness, adds 'but we do not know how far he penetrated.' She concludes by saying, 'Now that the battle has died down, the whole dossier of Rouffignac deserves to be re-examined calmly and objectively. That the immense prestige and authority of the Abbé Breuil, placed without reserve on the side of authenticity, should have caused the scale containing the speleologists to kick the beam is not surprising. One can only say, with great respect for the weight of his opinion, that those of us who know ourselves to be lesser fry by comparison are not thereby absolved or debarred from trying to form our own judgement in this puzzling case.'

Miss Garrod was writing in 1958. In the following year Professor Vaufrey wrote of the Rouffignac paintings, 'leur authenticité n'est pas douteuse' (*L'Anthropologie*, 1959, p. 370), but in the very same week one of the most distinguished living French archaeologists wrote to me, 'You know that Rouffignac is considered a scandalous fake. This will be another Glozel.' The Abbé Breuil died in the fullness of years in 1961, mourned by all who understood the enormous role he had played for so long in the development of Palaeolithic studies and particularly the discovery and study of Upper Palaeolithic art. In his obituary notice of the Abbé in *The Guardian* for 22 August 1961, Darsie Gillie, Paris correspondent of *The Guardian* and himself keenly interested in archaeology, said of the Abbé that he 'failed to carry conviction with many competent prehistorians when he declared authentic all the paintings in the Rouffignac caves. When the Académie des Inscriptions of which he was a member declined to discuss a communication he made on this subject . . . he swept out in a memorable whirlwind of soutane', and 'did not take his seat again for a long time.'

Rouffignac is still, then, the centre of controversy and there seems no obvious way of resolving it. The technical evidence, unfortunately, gets us nowhere. The Abbé Breuil summarized this in his paper on Rouffignac in the French archaeological publication *Gallia* (1957, fascicule 3, 1 ff.) but it does not provide convincing proof of authenticity or of non-authenticity. If only, as so many people have said to me when I have talked to them about these problems, there was some fool-proof scientific technique like C14 dating that could tell us the date of the paint used! But apparently there is not; the paints used are the pigments that would have been used in 20,000 B.C. and would have been used by a man in the twentieth century trying to reproduce these paintings. While the technical evidence is inconclusive, the subjective judgement of experts and art-historians and archaeologists continues to get us to diametrically opposed conclusions, some saying 'all is authentic,' others saying 'all is bogus.' Many French archaeologists refuse to discuss the matter either because it is not in their view worthy of discussion, or because they do not want to show their hands.

In their *The Caves of France and Northern Spain* (London, 1962) Ann and Gale Sieveking are clearly unhappy about the authenticity of the Rouffignac paintings; they describe them as 'rather pedestrian', and add 'if authentic'. Mademoiselle de St-Mathurin, in reviewing the Sieveking book, describes it thus: 'A rather guarded account of Rouffignac suggests that the authors recognize that its authenticity is not yet proved, an opinion in which the reviewer concurs' (*Antiquity*, 1963, 71–2). But on the other hand other recent books on Palaeolithic art such as A. Laming-Emperaire's *La Signification de l'Art Rupestre Paléolithique* (Paris, 1962), the volume entitled *The Art of the Stone Age: Forty Thousand Years of Rock Art* (London, 1961) written by Bandi, Breuil, Berger-Kirchner, Lhote, Holm and Lommel, and Lantier's *L'Art Préhistorique* (Paris, 1961) have no doubts whatsoever about Rouffignac.

When I came to revise this book for present-day publication I realized that Rouffignac would be a problem. I knew that some ill-informed people regard me as a party to the dispute merely because I have tried honestly to set out the differing views about the site and because I am not (or not yet) convinced of its authenticity *in toto*. It would have been possible to include no reference to the site or to put a discussion of Rouffignac in an appendix: both courses would be dishonest and cowardly. Let us face the issue boldly. A lot of people think Rouffignac is all right; a lot of people are still very doubtful. I personally have a great regard for the judgement of men like Breuil and Graziosi; but no less a regard for the judgement of women like Dorothy Garrod and Suzanne de St-Mathurin. I have what Graziosi demands of one, namely, 'normal experience of pre-historic art', and it makes me unhappy, stylistically, about the paintings on the Grand Plafond. I am also quite unable at present to set aside the evidence of Martel, Peyrony, Pierret, William Martin and the Cambridge speleologists of 1939. Forgeries can and do happen, great men can and do make mistakes, and equally, people can and do visit sites and not notice what is there!

So whether Rouffignac is to be on the list with Glozel and Piltdown, or on the list with Altamira and Lascaux, it had to come in and be dealt with in this book. And it had to be dealt with at considerable length because the issues are complex. But this book is not a treatise on Rouffignac: it is a guide to some aspects of the archaeology of France. Visit the site after reading this chapter and having first seen the great sites at Les Eyzies and Lascaux; and remember that there was a time when people tried to make out that Lascaux was a forgery! Read some of the books and articles about the site that we have mentioned, and think of all these things as Monsieur Plassard takes you round in his little train. Try and make up your mind. It is difficult. When I last saw the site in September, 1962, Monsieur Plassard, who knows well I did not sign either of the 1956 declarations, asked me whether I was convinced. The answer is No, I am not. I am *still* puzzled by Rouffignac, still trying to get the rights and wrongs sorted out. I would like to see an international commission go into the whole affair, just as it did at Glozel, but it may now be too late to do this.

Rouffignac has been classed a *monument historique* by the French Government, and rightly so. It certainly *is* a historic

3. (a) The quayside at St-Cado

3. (b) A fishing port in southern Brittany

14. Oblique air view of the Carnac alignments

15. (a) Part of the Carnac alignments

15. (b) Stone rows at Lagatjar

site whether it be a complete forgery, completely authentic or—that most difficult and worrying solution—a site that originally contained genuine ancient paintings and has had others added in an imitative style. I wish I knew the answer. I have always been impressed by what the Abbé Breuil generously called 'the very legitimate doubts of M. Pierret and his fellow cave-explorers'. Just as the manuscript of this book is going to press (June, 1963) I have heard again from William Martin and Bernard Pierret about their legitimate doubts. Martin recently visited Rouffignac and writes, 'C'est une honte d'abuser ainsi la crédulité des gens, avec une abondance de dessins et gravures qui, je suis formel, n'existaient pas en 1948.' Bernard Pierret's careful testimony amounts to this: (1) there were paintings when he and his colleagues first visited Rouffignac in 1945, and he particularly recalls those on the Grand Plafond, (2) during their visits to the cave between 1945 and 1949 paintings appeared progressively and in places where they knew that the walls hitherto had been blank—and one of these areas was the wall with its frieze of rhinoceroses, (3) when in 1949 Pierret and his colleagues discussed the paintings with Severin Blanc he said that *all* of them were false. Pierret does *not* agree with this view, regarding most of them as authentic.

We then seem to be presented with three points of view about Rouffignac: first, the Nougier-Robert point of view which declares that everything at Rouffignac is authentic, supported by the Abbé Breuil, Professor Almagro, Professor Graziosi and many others; second, the Pierret point of view, that some authentic paintings were there in 1945 but that many fakes were painted on the walls between 1945 and 1949; and, third, the point of view taken by Severin Blanc in public, and in private by many others, namely that what Pierret saw in 1945 was merely evidence that what he saw going on between 1945 and 1949 had already begun, and that *all* the paintings and engravings are modern. There it is. I would like to know the answer and so would the reader of this book. If I knew it myself with anything approaching certainty I would not have ended this chapter with, figuratively, a large question mark.

❧ VII ❧

More Caves and Rock Shelters

W e have so far concentrated on the Les Eyzies-
Montignac area of the Dordogne because this is the
classic area for studying Palaeolithic art, and this
was the primary purpose of this book when first written—to
provide an introduction to the study of caves and of megaliths
by concentrating on the two richest areas of the Dordogne and
the Morbihan. But there are many more painted and engraved
Palaeolithic caves in France than those within a few miles of
Les Eyzies and Montignac; the total number in France is
somewhere between 70 and 80 and the details of them all can
be found in two books, the Abbé Breuil's *Four Hundred Centuries
of Cave Art* published in 1952 and *The Caves of France and Northern
Spain* by Ann and Gale Sieveking published ten years later. We
have already referred to these books; the Abbé's book is large—
the Sieveking book is small and ideal for the pocket, the knap-
sack, the car: both are indispensable.

My purpose in this chapter is just to indicate the areas where
cave-hunting can be carried out. There are in France four areas
as follows: (1) from Poitiers to Périgueux, (2) to the south of
Sarlat and Souillac and between these towns and Cahors,
(3) south-eastern France, or rather the lower Rhône valley
from Montélimar to Nîmes; and (4) the foothills of the Pyrenees
from Foix on the east to Biarritz on the west. I now propose to
mention some of the most worth-while sites to visit in these four
groups (Map 3).

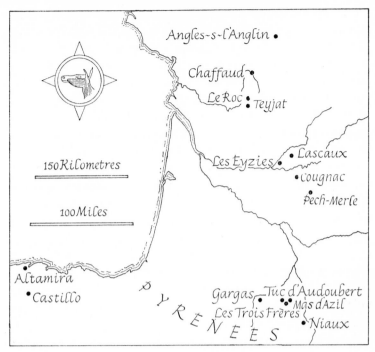

Map 3. Some other prehistoric sites with palaeolithic art in south-western France and northern Spain

1. POITIERS TO PÉRIGUEUX

Angles-sur-L'Anglin is a small town thirty miles from Poitiers and just over twenty miles from Chatellerault. The Sorcerer's Rock overlooks the river L'Anglin about a quarter of a mile from the town. Since the last war paintings and engravings and sculptures have been found here by Mademoiselle de St-Mathurin and Dr Dorothy Garrod. They are Magdalenian in date and include a fine frieze of sculptured animals, three 'Venus' figures, the painted portrait of a man and a sculptured and painted head of an ibex. The last two fine things are in the Musée de l'Homme in Paris. The site itself is closed to visitors, except by very special arrangement, at present (1963), but when the St-Mathurin-Garrod excavations are completed it will be put in order by the Beaux-Arts and be visitable. It will be very well worth while making a special visit for anyone driving to the Dordogne by a western route.

South of Angoulême and on the same western route there are three sites worth a visit. Moutiers-sur-Boeme is a small town ten miles south-west of Angoulême. There is a large paper mill in the valley bottom and behind this mill is La Chaire-à-Calvin, a rock-shelter with a frieze of sculptured animals—horses and an ox. The Roc de Sers is a rock-shelter in the small village of Sers just over ten miles south-east of Angoulême. Excavations revealed a frieze of sculptured animals some of which had fallen into the prehistoric deposits of the cave and could thus be dated to Upper Solutrean times. These sculptures are now in the Musée des Antiquités Nationales at St-Germain-en-Laye; casts of some of them have been set up in the rock-shelter itself. Teyjat is twenty odd miles from Angoulême on the road to Nontron. The cave, called La Mairie, is in the centre of the village behind the school; the key must be obtained from the village blacksmith. Here we find a series of fine engravings on stalagmite near the entrance of the cave and these include oxen, horses, cave-bears and reindeer. Some of the engravings on stalagmite were broken off and were discovered buried in the Magdalenian V/VI deposits of the cave.

2. From Sarlat to Cahors

Fifteen miles south of Sarlat and near the town of Gourdon is the cave of Cougnac discovered in 1952. It has an interesting and important collection of paintings believed to belong to the Aurignacian-Périgordian style. They include mammoth, ibex, elk and deer but the most interesting are paintings of human figures pierced by lances.

Cahors is a most attractive town, forty-five miles south of Sarlat. It is set on a horseshoe bend of the River Lot and is the ancient capital of Quercy. The Cathedral and the fourteenth-century fortified Pont Valentré—one of the most photographed bridges in France—should be seen as well as the old town with its narrow twisting streets. I have eaten well in Cahors in La Taverne—*truffes en croustade* and *coquelet à la broche*—and drunk there and elsewhere in Quercy the local red wine named after the town. Cahors is a robust fruity wine with a rich dark colour and a dryish astringent after-taste. Take a glass of it after you have visited the cave of Pech-Merle at Cabrerets which is twenty miles east of Cahors.

Pech-Merle was discovered in 1920 by the Abbé Lemozi who was led to it by a young child in his parish by name André David. The child had explored the cave himself previously. It is one of the largest prehistoric painted caves and one of the finest. There are horses and mammoths and cattle, and many representations of stencilled hands and strange outline drawings of human beings.

3. The Lower Rhône Valley

Here, in the lower Rhône valley, between Montélimar and Nîmes, three sites deserve a visit for those who are devoted hunters of Palaeolithic cave art. The first is Ebbou at Vallon in the Ardèche some twenty miles from Pont-St-Esprit. The art here was not discovered until 1947 and consists of horses, oxen, deer, ibex and mammoth—all engravings. These are in a style slightly different from the art of the classic Dordogne area or for that matter the whole of western France and northern Spain in general. It is more allied to engravings found in Sicily and elsewhere in the last fifteen years and belongs to a Mediterranean rather than to a Franco-Cantabrian school of Upper Palaeolithic art. Bayol is at Collias near Remoulins and the Pont du Gard and is fifteen miles from Nîmes. It contains some positive hand imprints in red paint and some animal paintings of ibex and horse. The third interesting site in this area is Baume Latrone, ten miles north of Nîmes—a huge cave opening off the gorge of the river Gardon. The most interesting art here is a decoration of stylized animal figures drawn with fingers dipped in wet clay.

But it must be said in all fairness that Ebbou, Bayol and Baume Latrone are more for specialist archaeological travellers than

the generality of those interested in the major works of Palaeolithic art. Indeed I should not blame the archaeological traveller
who prefers the Roman remains at Nîmes and Arles to these
caves and lingers at the Pont du Gard and Orange and Avignon.
The real interest of course is Ebbou, providing as it does the best
example so far of the Mediterranean style of Upper Palaeolithic
art in France.

4. THE FRENCH PYRENEES

We turn to our last group, the caves in the foothills of the
French Pyrenees, and here we are back in an area which is
only second to the Dordogne in its intrinsic interest and importance. The easiest way to see some of the great Pyrenean
sites is from Toulouse. Drive south up the valley of the Ariège
to Foix via Pamiers. Toulouse to Pamiers is forty miles and
from this very agreeable little town on to Foix is about eleven
miles. Stay in Foix at the Hostellerie Barbacane or ten miles
farther on at Tarascon-sur-Ariège (the Poste and the Francal
have both been strongly recommended to me) or at the Eychenne
at St-Girons, under thirty miles west of Foix. All this country
in the triangle between Pamiers and Foix, and Tarascon on the
east, Mas d'Azil and St-Girons on the west and Massat on the
south is a paradise for game and venison; at the right times of
the year you can expect to taste *civet de chevreuil*, ptarmigan,
red partridge, larks (one of the specialities of the Barbacane at
Foix is *alouettes fourrées au foie gras*) and on very rare occasions
civet d'isard (the mountain chamois of the Pyrenees) and the
wild bear of Mas d'Azil—not to be obtained in restaurants.

Mas d'Azil is on the main road from Pamiers to St-Girons
(N.117). South of the town the road follows the river through
the hillside and in the middle of this tunnel there is an entrance
to a gallery containing prehistoric engravings including two
fine bison. This site is more famous for its *art mobilier* and we
include a photograph of a decorated spear-thrower from this
site (Plate 11). This belongs to the Magdalenian period. The
culture that succeeded the Magdalenian here in the Pyrenees is
called Azilian after this site.

From Mas d'Azil it is no distance to Les Trois Frères and Le Tuc d'Audoubert near Montesquieu-Avantès. These caves are only three miles from St-Girons but they are privately owned and, in the interests of their preservation, can only be visited after very special arrangements are made with the owners. They are therefore, I am afraid, out for the ordinary traveller, and should not be included in any proposed itinerary. Yet this is sad: Les Trois Frères has probably the finest collection of engravings in any Palaeolithic cave, whereas Tuc d'Audoubert has in it two bison modelled in clay. But if we cannot easily visit these two caves we can at least appreciate the story of their discovery and indeed share vicariously in its excitement. The Count Henri Bégouën had an estate at Montesquieu-Avantès only a few miles from the Mas d'Azil tunnel. He had three sons, Max, Jacques and Louis, and in 1912 the three brothers Bégouën explored the river Volp as it ran underground in a home-made boat made of boxes and petrol-tins. Max Bégouën had the idea that a curtain of stalagmite might be closing a narrow passage leading to a further cave. He broke through it and found an inner hall where, against a rock, there were leaning two bison realistically modelled in clay.

Later the three brothers explored the whole of the great cave, lowering themselves into a second cave below. They completed their explorations of this second cave during military leave in June, 1918. The caves of Trois Frères and Tuc d'Audoubert which are now divided into two separate caverns were once a single cavern and the ancient course of the river Volp. What is perhaps most exciting at Les Trois Frères is the representations of the sorcerer figure—a masked man in animal clothing and significantly placed near a natural pulpit in the cave where a similarly masked figure could emerge in reality.

Almost as exciting as the story of the discovery of Les Trois Frères and Tuc d'Audoubert, if not more so, is the tale of the discovery of Montespan, a cave not far from the others and about fifteen miles from St-Girons. It was found by the celebrated French speleologist Norbert Casteret in 1923. He had to swim through a siphon to get to what is now generally referred to as the Casteret-Godin Gallery and here he found, in addition to many engravings, some clay models and low relief sculptures on the floor. All are incomplete. The most famous is that of a headless bear three feet long crouched on the ground with the real skull of a young bear found between its forepaws. There is a hole in the centre of its neck and it is suggested that the skull might have been fastened to the clay model with a wooden pin and that the model itself which has a rubbed appearance might have been covered with a bear's skin. The bear's body has many holes where it had been stabbed. In another gallery at Montespan there are three or four horses represented with many holes pierced in their bodies. Surely here we are very close to the surviving material witness of Upper Palaeolithic ritual and hunting magic. Human footprints, some of them belonging to young people, have been found at Montespan, and at Tuc d'Audoubert there were marks of dancing footprints around the bison.

But alas, Montespan is even more difficult to visit than Les Trois Frères and the Tuc d'Audoubert; it can in fact only be visited by special arrangement with local archaeologists and by the use of very special equipment. Let us turn to the caves in this area which we can visit without any difficulty, namely Gargas, Marsoulas, and Niaux. Gargas is south of Montrejeau on the N. 117 road from St-Gaudens to Tarbes; it is famous for the very great number of stencilled hands painted on the walls —some of them apparently diseased or mutilated. Marsoulas is between St-Girons and Foix—a little village near Salies-du-Salat on N. 117. It has some fine engravings of horse, bison, ibex and reindeer and polychrome paintings much like Font de Gaume and Altamira in Spain.

Last, in this brief account of more caves to visit, is Niaux.[1]

---

[1] There are, by the way, four excellent little books produced in a series called *La Terre et l'Homme* (edited by Professor Louis-René Nougier) published by Edouard Privat of 14, Rue des Arts, Toulouse. They are guides to Pech-Merle, Gargas, Mas d'Azil, and Niaux. Each has a short text and a large number of excellent photographs including some in colour. When I bought my copies they were what is now 4 francs each—very good value indeed.

5. The Tumulus de St-Michel: (*a*) from the air

5. The Tumulus de St-Michel: (*b*) from the side

17. (a) The Table des Marchands at Locmariaquer

17. (b) Le Grand Menhir Brisé, Locmariaquer

In his *Four Hundred Centuries of Cave Art*, the Abbé Breuil referred to the six 'giants' among the painted and engraved caves. They were Altamira, Font de Gaume, Lascaux, Combarelles, Les Trois Frères, and Niaux. Altamira is in Spain and outside the scope of our present travels. We have seen Font de Gaume, Lascaux and Combarelles. We know that Les Trois Frères is difficult to see. We are left with the last great 'giant', namely Niaux. The cave of Niaux is between two and three miles from Tarascon-sur-Ariège. You visit it by making arrangements in the Syndicat d'Initiative at Tarascon. Having done this you set off with your guide and your equipment of acetylene lamps and the rest of it. It is a steep climb up to the entrance of the cave. The cave itself is a long one—it is over half a mile from the entrance to the famous Salon Noir. No visit to a Palaeolithic cave can be hurried, but you should be warned that Niaux takes four hours—a long, whole morning. The Salon Noir is so called because of its collection of extremely fine paintings in black outline which include twenty-five bison, sixteen horses, six ibexes, and one reindeer, several of the paintings being superimposed (Plate 12). There are many other things of interest in Niaux—the engraving of a bison pierced by three arrows, and some fish. But the clear bold lines of the black outline paintings of the Salon Noir are what gives one the most lasting impression of Niaux and it is a splendid way to end any tour of French cave art. Walk out of the dark cave and down the hillside to Tarascon, sit at a café and order a bottle of Blanquette de Limoux (if you are inclined to favour sweet luscious sparkling wines, which I am not) or Corbières rouge if you prefer a strong, dry, red wine as I do.

Anyhow, whatever your choice, you have earned your glass or your bottle: after those hours in the darkness of the hillside you can sit down to enjoy a good Ariégeois lunch—*foie gras*, an *omelette aux truffes*, and a *confit d'oie* or *de canard*. How curious that the food here should be so like what we would expect to eat after visiting Lascaux, Font de Gaume and Les Combarelles.

But of course there is no reason why a tour of Upper Palaeolithic art should end in Foix or Tarascon-sur-Ariège. There is all Spain and particularly the north. Cross the frontier and drive west along the Cantabrian coast to see Castillo, La Pasiega, Covalanas, Santián, Pindal, Hornos de la Peña, and the last and first of the six great 'giants'—Altamira. But that journey is another day. Here we have been interested in some of the highlights of French prehistory and must now turn from the Palaeolithic artists to the megalith builders.

✤ VIII ✤

Getting to Carnac

WE have spent enough time in the Dordogne, and should have a reasonable idea of its resources for understanding Upper Palaeolithic man. We must now turn to the other main area for the field archaeology of pre-historic times in France—namely, the Carnac area of the Morbihan. If you have first visited the Dordogne and are going on to Brittany, the journey by road is pleasant and not long. You make for Nantes, crossing the Loire by the first bridge, or for St-Nazaire, crossing it by ferry from Minden. My choice of route by road would be Angoulême and then through Cognac and Saintes to La Rochelle, and I would not hurry through Cognac, but pause and visit one or two of the great brandy houses to inspect the process of maturing cognac—and, of course, for a *dégustation*.

By train it is possible to leave Bordeaux at 13.24 (Train 912) and be at Nantes at 18.30; you change there and at Redon getting to Auray at nine o'clock in the evening. The same con-venient cross-country expresses serve you if you visit Brittany first and the Dordogne afterwards. You can leave Auray at 10.49 or Vannes at 11.07 (Train 708), and, changing at Nantes on to Train 909, leave after an hour for lunch at 13.55 getting to Bordeaux at 19.42. If you are going straight to Carnac from England you can go by boat to St-Malo, or by air to St-Malo Dinard, and the journey across is not long. The train will take you to Vannes, or Auray, or if you change to the Quiberon express, to the station of Plouharnel-Carnac. From any of these points you can travel by bus to Carnac or whatever centre you have chosen in the Morbihan—the departmental railway, alas! is no more. Your car can go by boat to St-Malo or Le Havre, or by air to Cherbourg, and, in the summer, Deauville. The routes across from Cherbourg and Deauville are full of pleasant things to see—Coutances Cathedral, Mont-St-Michel, Dol, Dinan, Rennes itself, and if you come from Deauville or Le Havre the D-Day beaches and Mulberry Harbour of north Normandy and the beautifully displayed embroidery at Bayeux—the so-called Bayeux Tapestry.

There is now a very good restaurant at Le Havre, the Monaco, where I dined on New Year's Eve, 1962, and while admiring the great *pièces montées* they had prepared for the *réveillon*, enjoyed an excellent meal of *bouquet rose* and *rognons flambés à la fine champagne*. Two other places to be remembered between Normandy and Brittany are Chez Léopold at Boulon south of Caen (the Rabelais at Caen is also good), and the Cheval Blanc at Vire. The Cheval Blanc at Vire has had a great reputation for a long time and may now be resting a little on it; it suffers from the disadvantage of all Vire of having been bombed in the 1939–45 War and entirely reconstructed, and I do not like the new French post-war hotels. But Madame Delaunay's high tradition of cookery continues at the Cheval Blanc and I was delighted the other day to eat there her *Bonhomme Normand*, duckling flamed in calvados served on a purée of apples—a really memorable dish.

A drive across Brittany would include the late sixteenth-century Calvary of Guéhenno—one of the best in the province —the château of Josselin, and Vannes itself. The great moment comes as you press south by train or car or bus and you arrive on the sandy heaths of the Morbihan—the *Landes des Megalithes*; there, against the evening sun, are the dark silhouettes of pine trees and a chambered tomb. Not far away is the sea, with sailing boats and yachts tossing at anchor, and a cosy bar where a dozen oysters and half a bottle of Muscadet are waiting for you.

If you want to get to the Morbihan in a great hurry, the best way is to fly to Paris or go to Paris overnight. It is then possible to leave Paris Montparnasse at 9.00, reaching Auray at 16.31.

Similarly, on the return, the Paris train leaves Auray at 10.26 to arrive at Montparnasse at 18.15. But let us have done with these details; half an hour with the *Indicateur Chaix* or a letter to the French Railway Office[1] will resolve your difficulties. Let us suppose you have got to Carnac, and have degusted your oysters and Muscadet. Now look around you.

The village of Carnac itself has little to interest us except the remains of prehistory. It is a very ordinary west French village with a population at the present day of just over 3,000 inhabitants; perhaps, as some of the guide-books do, it should be described as a small town. It lies about a mile from the sea, from which it is separated by a flat, sandy heath overgrown with pines and now covered in a rash of small villas—the villas of the *estivants*, or summer visitors, who are concentrated on Carnac-Plage. Perhaps the best way to describe Carnac-Plage is in the inimitable words of the tourist pamphlet, *Carnac; Au Pays des Megalithes; Carnac-Plage—Reine du Morbihan*. This is what the current pamphlet says about the Queen of the Morbihan in its own splendid *Syndicat d'Initiative* English:

> Carnac is comprising in two parts: Carnac Town and Carnac Beach. . . . Carnac Beach, climateric and seaside well known Place, is enlarging every year, owing to it privileged altitude. . . . Carnac Beach, in the middle of trees, with shady avenues, hotels, villas, cottages, storehouses, is the most attractive Briton shore. The sandy beach, long of two miles, with a gentle slope, is of all tranquillity for children and baths can be taken at any hour of tide. Sunlight is great and by the arborescent climate, mimosas, eucalyptus, and camelias trees are growing in profusion.

Well, there you have it. And if you want a privileged altitude, tranquillity for children, and an arborescent climate, go to Carnac-Plage. I have never stayed there, but have often bathed 'at any hour of tide' along the two sandy miles of its 'most attractive Briton shore'; and 'a most attractive Briton shore' it is. Some of my most pleasant memories of Carnac are of walks

[1] The French Railway Office and the French Tourist Office at 179 Piccadilly, London, W.1, are only too delighted to supply information about trains and hotels.

in the dusk from Carnac to the beach through the pine woods, with glow-worms a-tail-glowing, and the warm sea cool after hot July days.

I have been quoting from an old brochure but the current tourist literature of Carnac is equally pleasant. It calls Carnac 'la reine du Morbihan', and the centre of 'la terre du Passé'. I should here issue a warning about the season for travelling to the Morbihan. It is delightful in the summer, of course, and all the hotel facilities are available from Easter to the end of September. The winter is not the time for megalith-hunting in Brittany. I have spent two Christmases in the Morbihan; both were described as exceptional, and in cafés the constant talk was of the unusual *verglas* and the abnormal conditions. Of course, as elsewhere in France, the inside of the hotels that are open in the winter is cosy and warm—too warm, often—and the food as good as it always is, but the winter megalithing is for the specialists and *aficianados*. Carnac-Plage itself is a sad sight at Christmas time—hotels with shuttered windows, closed cafés, and deserted notices advertising those useful 'professors' that flourish on French beaches teaching your children how to swim and ride and slide down things and offering you massage and physical culture.

Carnac-Plage is laid out with roads parallel to and at right angles to the beach, and the names of these roads have a very megalithic flavour: the Rue des Menhirs, for example, or the Rue des Alignements, or the Rue du Tumulus, which cuts through the Avenue des Druides. So does the Rue du Dolmen —and there really is a dolmen in Carnac-Plage, underneath the pine trees and sandwiched between *pensions* and postcard shops. If you drove from the Dordogne through St-Nazaire you may have seen the dolmen there; it is one of the few towns that has a megalithic monument in the middle of it—a small one, admittedly, but a dolmen for all that.

The word 'dolmen' needs some explanation here. Indeed, now is the moment, as we sit on the beach at Carnac-Plage, to consider the whole problem of the classification and nomenclature of megalithic monuments. Very broadly, we can divide these prehistoric monuments into three categories: first, those consisting of single stones; second, those consisting of several single stones grouped together in horizontal arrangements, such as circles and rows; and, third, those consisting of stones grouped together in horizontal and vertical arrangements to make rooms or chambers. The first class, the single standing stone, is usually referred to as the *menhir*, which literally means 'long stone'. The second class is usually referred to by descriptive names, such as circles and rows or alignments, and one of the main reasons for coming to this part of the Morbihan is to see the great Carnac alignments. The third class of monument is the most widespread in western Europe; there must be well over 20,000 of these megalithic chambers still in existence. We shall meet these megalithic chambers in the Carnac region in two forms, sometimes free-standing like this one at Carnac-Plage, and sometimes buried in a mound or cairn or tumulus of earth and stones. It seems likely that most of these megalithic chambers were originally covered by mounds or tumuli—indeed, they would not have made very adequate tombs if they were not so covered. The free-standing chambers are thus denuded chambered tumuli, and as you travel about the Morbihan you will see all stages in the denudation of these tumuli: from great high mounds, to mounds 2 or 3 feet high around the feet of the stones, to monuments that are apparently completely free of any mound.

These burial chambers, whether in mounds or free-standing, have always been impressive and notable features of the Breton landscape, and there, as now in most of France, the word 'dolmen' has been used for some time as a general descriptive term for them. This is a difficult word in that its derivation is not certain, and in that it has been used by scholars outside France for a special kind of megalithic monument. The great Swedish archaeologist Oscar Montelius devised a threefold classification of megalithic burial chambers, and his first class was translated into English, rather unhappily, as the 'dolmen' class, so that in English books about Scandinavian archaeology you will see reference to the Dolmen Age or Dolmen Period, or to dolmens as only one type of megalithic tomb. Here in Brittany the best thing is to follow current French usage and to use the term 'dolmen' as a general term for any megalithic tomb. 'Où se trouve le dolmen?' is a perfectly reasonable request to make to anyone in the Morbihan, and they will direct you to the burial chamber you are looking for. In a country where there are such things as a Hôtel des Dolmens and Cafés des Dolmens as well as Rues des Dolmens, it would seem pedantic to do other than use it as a generic term for megalithic tombs.

In south-west England we have a word which is rather close etymologically to 'dolmen'; and this is 'tolven', or holed stone. There is a Tolven and a Men-an-tol in Cornwall, but the word 'dolmen' does not exist as a common folk-name for megalithic chambers in England and Wales; I do not think you would get much further if you asked in Pembrokeshire or the Cotswolds to be directed to the dolmen. In Wales the common folk-name for a burial chamber is 'cromlech'; this word is worth remembering here, because in Brittany stone circles and stone squares of megaliths are referred to as cromlechs. This is just one more of these tantalizing confusions which bedevil the nomenclature of megalithic monuments.

Let us turn our back on the megaliths for a moment and look out to sea. The view is a good one. On the west the Peninsula of Quiberon, with Quiberon itself at the end—an important pleasure resort and sardine-tinning port. It is from Quiberon that the steamers go across to Belle Ile, which you can see in the distance, and then in the middle distance are the little islands of Houat and Hoedic. Carnac is really the north point of the Bay of Quiberon, and this is a bay famous in history for at least two reasons. First, it was probably the scene of the action between Caesar's *triremes* and the Veneti in 56 B.C. Julius Caesar's conquest of Gaul took place between 58 and 50 B.C. In 57 B.C. he overcame almost all the Belgic tribes in the north; the tribes of Normandy and Brittany submitted without a fight, and by the end of the year almost the whole of Gaul between the Garonne and the Rhine was under Roman control. During the next six years of the war the main events in Gaul were the crushing of four rebellions by various groups of tribes. The first to rebel were the Veneti and other tribes on the Atlantic coast; this was in 56 B.C. The Veneti lived in the Morbihan and their name survives in the capital city of Vannes. They were described by Caesar as the most powerful tribe on the west coast, with a large fleet of ships, in which they traded with Britain. Having decided to fight the Romans, they fortified their strongholds, stocked them with corn from the fields and got together as many ships as they could on the coast. The Veneti lived in what modern archaeologists call promontory forts, or, at least, used these as strongholds when attacked. Caesar says that most of their strongholds were so situated on the ends of spits or headlands that it was impossible to approach them by land: and that when the defence of these was hopeless the defenders brought up ships and retired to a neighbouring stronghold equally well protected.

'They found it easy to pursue these tactics', wrote Caesar, 'because our ships were weatherbound and sailing was very hazardous in that vast, open sea, where the tides were high and harbours almost non-existent.' Caesar described the Venetic ships as flat-bottomed, with exceptionally high bows and sterns and hulls entirely of oak: 'The anchors were secured with iron chains instead of ropes. They used sails made of raw hides or thin leather, either because they had no flax and were ignorant of its use, or more probably because they thought that ordinary sails would not stand the violent storms and squalls of the Atlantic and were not suitable for such heavy vessels.'

Caesar decided that he could not defeat the Veneti except in a sea-battle. Two hundred and twenty Venetic ships were engaged. They could not be rammed, but were defeated by the use of pointed hooks fixed into the end of long poles; with these the halyards were grasped and pulled taut, and then snapped by rowing hard away. This brought the yards down and the Venetic ships were immobilized. The Veneti were destroyed, and the whole naval action apparently took place not far from the coast 'under the eyes of Caesar and the whole army. . . . All the cliffs and hills that commanded a near view of the sea were occupied by the troops.' There is no certainty where this remarkable action took place, but the general consensus of opinion is that it was in the Bay of Quiberon, and as I have looked out over the still waters of the bay I have often thought of it—of the Venetic battle and also of that other extraordinary engagement that took place here in June, 1795, when 6,000 French *émigrés*, some of them *ci-devant* noblemen, and others who were supposed to be converted Republican prisoners, were disembarked at the base of the Quiberon Peninsula under the protection of Commodore Warren's squadron. They were joined by bands of *Chouans*—peasant supporters of the royalist cause who imitated the cry of an owl (*chat-huant*) as a signal on their expeditions. In spite of brave resistance, the invading force was driven back into the sea and obliged to surrender. The English ships were driven off shore in a storm. A statue of General Hoche at Quiberon commemorates this engagement, and at Port Haliguen is a pyramid marking the spot where the *émigrés* laid down their arms.

But let us leave these memories of old naval engagements, and leave too the bathing huts and villas and hotel terraces of Carnac-Plage. Let us leave the *estivants* to their *apéritifs* and the sea, and return to Carnac itself, which was famous as a tourist resort for its megalithic monuments before ever bathing in the sea became fashionable. The village itself has a church built in the seventeenth century dedicated to St-Cornély—St. Cornelius, the patron saint of horned cattle in Brittany. St-Cornély is represented by a statue on the façade of the church, set between two oxen. The church has a curious stone baldaquin over the porch; it is in the form of a crown, and no other comparable examples are known in Brittany. The village legend has it that this great stone porch roof is built from menhirs and that the altar of the church is also built from dolmens. Both these stories may well be true. The Church of St-Cornély has a pleasant and attractive spire; inside, the slanting beams of the nave and aisles are decorated with seventeenth-century paintings. There is a fountain dedicated to St-Cornély to the west of the church. His pardon is on the second Sunday in September. It is accompanied by a fair held on 13 September, when the cattle are drawn up in a semicircle before the church, presented, and then blessed. The animals are then driven in procession through the streets. During this interesting pardon and fair some people offer to St-Cornély a tuft of hair taken from the tails of their cows.[1]

St-Cornély and the cows on the Church front at Carnac

As our main interest in Carnac is its prehistoric archaeology we turn first to the Museum, which is not far from the church on the road to La-Trinité-sur-Mer. The Museum is now called the Musée Archéologique James Miln-Zacharie le Rouzic, and by this name commemorates the two men who founded it and

[1] For these and other legends and folk-tales see Z. Le Rouzic, *Carnac; Légendes, Traditions, Coutumes et Contes du Pays* (Rennes; first published 1909; revised current edition).

brought it to fame. James Miln (1818–81) was a Scotsman who
had travelled widely and lived long in China, India and New
Zealand. He was a man of fifty when he first visited Brittany;
this was in 1873. He came to Carnac and fell in love with the
country; the great stone monuments excited his interest, his
imagination and his curiosity. One day he was walking in a
field called Le Bossenno, which some people persisted in referring to as the Camp de César. Miln was excited by the in-
equalities of the ground, which he thought obviously covered
some hidden buildings. As he walked over the fields he picked
up bits of pottery and tesserae from mosaic pavements. Miln
saw here a chance to establish the relation of the alignments
nearby to what were obviously Roman remains at Le Bossenno.
At this time the date of the alignments and of megalithic monuments in general was much in discussion. Miln decided to
excavate at Carnac. He was in good health, with nothing to do,
with plenty of money and a passion for original research. He
was like his contemporary, Colonel Lane-Fox, who, the year
before Miln was to die, inherited the Pitt-Rivers estates in
Cranborne Chase, and, also with nothing particular to do,
plenty of money and a passion for original research, began a
remarkable series of excavations which revealed him as a
pioneer of archaeological technique and, in the words of Sir
Mortimer Wheeler, 'the greatest of all archaeological excavators.'

James Miln was not comparable in his excavational technique with General (Lane-Fox) Pitt-Rivers, but he worked with
great energy and interest. He began digging at Le Bossenno in
1874 and worked there for three seasons uncovering what was
a Roman villa.[1] His results were published in 1877 simul-
taneously in French in Paris and in English in Edinburgh under
the title of *Excavations at Carnac: A Record of Archaeological Researches in the Bossenno and the Mont St. Michel.* The book published, Miln still could not leave Carnac, which he made his
headquarters. He went on digging and exploring, and in 1881

---

[1] This site has now been destroyed, and there is nothing to see at Le
Bossenno.

published his second book, *Excavations at Carnac: Archaeological Researches in the Alignments of Kermario*. He had just finished correcting the proofs when he was taken ill. He died as the book was being printed.

Miln had lived all his eight years at Carnac in the Hôtel des Voyageurs: the small rooms which served him as bedroom and study were piled high with excavated material. He had expressed a wish that all this should be left to the commune of Carnac. His brother and legatee, Robert Miln, fulfilled this wish and built the little Museum which still bears the name of James Miln.

The other name which the Museum bears is one that is very common in the Morbihan, the name of Le Rouzic. Zacharie Le Rouzic was born in 1864, the youngest of a family of nine children; his father was a weaver. He left school at ten and was chosen by James Miln to accompany him on his field-work trips and to carry his paint-box. When James Miln died and his brother set up the Carnac Museum, Zacharie Le Rouzic was appointed first guardian of the Museum, and he remained in charge from the age of seventeen until he died in 1939, a distinguished and much-loved old man of seventy-five. During the nearly sixty years of his curatorship of the Museum he conducted a great number of excavations in megalithic tombs, in habitation sites, and in all kinds of prehistoric sites. He published a short guide, *Les monuments mégalithiques de Carnac et de Locmariaquer; leur destination, leur âge*, which first appeared in 1897. It was also published in English, and a revised French edition can be bought in the Musée Miln-Le Rouzic at the present day as well as the Catalogue of the Museum, first published in 1894. Le Rouzic wrote a very great deal on the Morbihan megaliths and on the prehistory of the Morbihan, and it was appropriate and just that at his death the Museum was rechristened the Musée Miln-Le Rouzic. The present curator is Maurice Jacq, Zacharie Le Rouzic's son-in-law.

I first met Zacharie Le Rouzic in the mid-thirties when I was an undergraduate, and, on several visits to Carnac in the six years before the outbreak of the 1939–45 War and Le Rouzic's death, had long talks with him and visited sites and his own excavations with him. He was interested in everything, from the first human beings in Brittany to modern Breton politics; but the megaliths were his main love. We discussed particularly the date of the megaliths. Miss V. C. C. Collum had excavated a megalithic tomb between St-Malo and Dinan and said that it was Gallo-Roman in date. She went further than this and claimed that probably all the megalithic monuments were Gallo-Roman in date and not prehistoric. The generally accepted date for them, according to most archaeologists at that time, was the first half of the second millennium B.C.—say between 2000 B.C. and 1500 B.C. Miss Collum proposed to make them 2,000 years later, and so completely to upset the whole chronological fabric of prehistory. It is true that Gallo-Roman finds are made in megalithic tombs. Miss Collum had been working with Le Rouzic on a corpus of megalithic tombs in the Morbihan, and he had to respect her energy and industry. I remember going over carefully with Le Rouzic all the dating evidence from the Morbihan tombs and coming to the conclusion that Miss Collum's thesis could not be sustained, and that the general view was the correct one.

There are many things to see in the Carnac Museum. Particular attention might be paid to two things: the first is the collection of megalithic art in the inner room, and the second is to this matter of chronology. As you travel about in the Morbihan you will see many examples of megalithic art, and if your tour is long enough to see Gavr'innis you will see one of the finest decorated megalithic monuments in the world. We can discuss this art when we get to some of the decorated tombs. At the moment a careful glance at the inner room in the Carnac Museum is to be recommended. Here are some original decorated stones which had to be moved for safety's sake from their original find-spots. Most of the exhibits, however, are casts and there are also casts of megalithic art from other areas in France—the Paris Basin, the Marne rock-cut tombs, and particularly the remarkable statue-menhirs of the south of France.

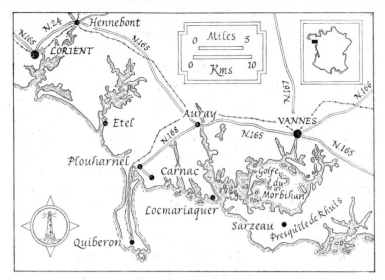

Map 4. Carnac, Locmariaquer and the Morbihan

The second point worth concentrating on is this matter of chronology. Even the most amateur of archaeologists as he walks round the cases in the Carnac Museum will recognize that from many megalithic tombs there comes a characteristic finely made red or red-brown pottery decorated with bands and incisions; this is what we call in English *beaker* or *bell-beaker* pottery and the French call *les vases caliciformes* or *campaniformes*. Radiocarbon analysis now suggests that the date of this pottery is somewhere in the period of 2000 to 1700 B.C. These megalithic tombs were being used if not built, then, at the beginning of the second millennium B.C. In addition to the Beakers there is one other exhibit in the Carnac Museum to look at with particular interest. It comes from the megalithic tomb known as Parc Guren II. Here in 1926, when Zacharie Le Rouzic was carrying out some excavations preparatory to reconstructing the tomb, he found sherds of bell-beaker, a broken triangular riveted copper dagger, and a small segmented bead of faience. Faience is a blue-green glass-like material; the word was originally used for a glazed ware made at Faenza in Italy, but is now used generally for many kinds of porcelain and glazed earthenware. The term is especially used for the glazed material manufactured a great deal by the ancient Egyptians. These segmented faience beads have been studied with the greatest care by archaeologists and chemists, and it seems likely that they were made in Egypt in the fourteenth century B.C., and traded through Europe, perhaps via Crete and Mycenae. Many are found in the British Isles, and the general presumption is that where they occur they date that particular archaeological level to the fourteenth or thirteenth century B.C.: we cannot be more accurate, because we do not know, for instance, how long these imported beads were kept in western Europe before they were lost or buried.

It is by no means certain that all the objects found at Parc Guren II were found in association; these megalithic burial chambers were used often as burial vaults over a long period of time, and it is not possible to be certain whether the objects found in them date from the first burial or from a later burial, or even of course from a later and secondary use of the tomb. The importance of Parc Guren is that here were bell-beaker sherds and a bead that can hardly be later than the thirteenth century B.C. Here at least is one megalithic tomb being used in the last quarter of the second millennium.

But when were these megalithic tombs first used, and when were the earliest of them built? Until recently the consensus of opinion has been that they did not date earlier than the end of the third millennium B.C., and in my *The Prehistoric Chamber Tombs of France* published as recently as 1960 the date there given for the earliest monuments was '*c.* 2300 to 2000 B.C.' But even as those words were being printed Carbon 14 dates were being obtained which suggested that most archaeologists who had been writing about megaliths up till then had been wrong and had too short a chronology. This is not the place to go into this complex matter, but it now appears that we must allow the possibility that the earliest tombs in Brittany were constructed even before 3000 B.C. This seems a guarded statement; we do have some Carbon 14 dates of this period for Breton tombs but

3. (*a*) The stone circles of Er-Lannic

3. (*b*) The Crucuno Dolmen, between Carnac and Erdeven

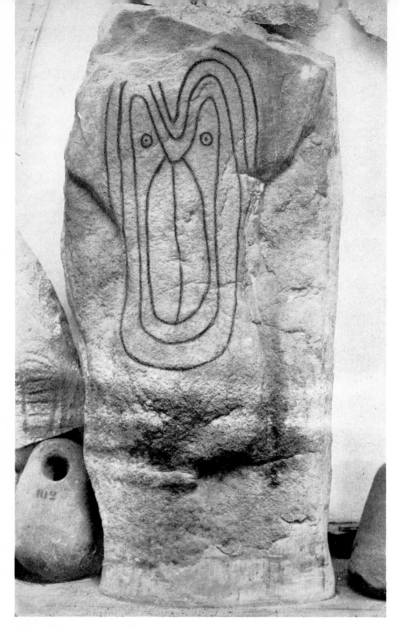

19. Stylized human figure from Luffang

we also have some other very strange dates. It does look however as though for the moment we should regard the period during which megalithic tombs were being built in France as from 3000 to 1500 B.C. (or even 1000 B.C.). This means of course that megalithic tombs and temples were used in France and in prehistoric western Europe for a very long time, and that the megalith builders were not a small unimportant group of people but perhaps one of the main formative elements in the peopling of prehistoric Iberia, France and the British Isles.[1]

We must now leave these theoretical issues and set out to see the megaliths, but before we do we must have somewhere to lay down our heads and somewhere to eat. There are several hotels in Carnac-Ville. James Miln spent all his days at the Hôtel des Voyageurs, which an old Murray Guide described as 'a humble and clean country inn' and which Augustus Hare in his *Carnac* (1892) described as 'homely, but good and comfortable: horse and chaise for hire'. I often stayed there; it was good and unpretentious and open all the year round, but alas it is no more—neither food nor drink, neither horse nor chaise. It closed down in 1961. There are now three hotels in Carnac-Ville, the de la Marine (with 30 rooms), the Hôtel des Dolmens (with 40 rooms), and the Hôtel des Alignements (with 12 rooms); all are open only in the season from Easter to the end of September. There is also the Hôtel du Tumulus on the hill above the town and just by the Tumulus de St-Michel from which it takes its name. It is run by Maurice Jacq Le Rouzic and his wife (son-in-law and daughter of the archaeologist) and is open from 15th June to 15th September. It is the hotel in which I first stayed as an undergraduate visiting Carnac thirty years ago and I treasure memories of its food and comfort and its wonderful view.

Carnac-Plage has many hotels ranging from the Britannia with 80 rooms to the Ker Ihuel with 28 and the Genets with 32. Information about all of them can be obtained from the

---

[1] For a discussion of these C14 dates and the 'new' chronology of megalithic tombs see P-R. Giot, *Brittany*, p. 54, and the French edition of this book (*Bretagne* (Paris, 1962), pp. 66–68, 76–77).

Syndicat d'Initiative of Carnac/Plouharnel, Avenue des Druides, Carnac. Farther afield Auray has a very well-known hotel, the Pavillon d'en Haut with 50 rooms and a quoted pension of 35 to 48 francs s.t.c. It is classified as a *bonne table* in the *Guide Kléber-Colombes* which lists its specialities as *palourdes grillées, filets de sole, homard pavillon,* and *beurre blanc nantais.* It is an old house that has been modernized and has a fine collection of Breton furniture and woodwork. Across the Place de la République from the Pavilion d'en Haut are the Moderne and the Croix Verte (a *routier* establishment)—both inexpensive and with cheap meals. The Moderne and the Croix Verte are the places for students and others on a tight budget.

Vannes used to have a large good hotel, the Dauphin, but this is now closed. The *Guide Michelin* lists several hotels (and the Vannes Syndicat d'Initiative is at 29, Rue Thiers) but I have heard personally recommended the Gare et Terminus opposite the station, with 46 rooms. The Marée Bleue, 8, Place Bir-Hakeim, has 23 rooms from 9 to 12 francs (with *pension* at 22 francs). I have never stayed there but often eaten in its restaurant and if the general arrangements correspond to the charm and good will of the restaurant it would be an excellent headquarters for a visit to the Morbihan. Madame Bodard is a splendid restaurateur and has an excellent chef who has many very fine dishes. One of these I remember especially well, namely his *brochette de coquille St-Jacques flambée à la champagne, sauce béarnaise;* I would go many a mile of a detour to eat this splendid *plat.* But it is the general value of the Marée Bleue that I recommend as much as (or more than) its high gastronomy. Here is its menu for a 6 francs meal at Christmas 1962: *paté, moules marinières, boeuf aux pruneaux* with *pommes à l'anglaise,* and a choice of desserts—surely very good value for nine shillings; and for those who still find France expensive what about this for value, the Marée Bleue's fifteen shillings Christmas Day lunch or dinner? I think this six-course meal could hardly be bettered for value anywhere, and for those who, like me, don't like the *bûche de Noël* there is a cheese board with always an excellent choice.

Huîtres Plates
Terrine de Gibier
Lieu sauce Hollandaise
Dinde aux Marrons
Salade
Bûche de Noël

There is another good restaurant in Vannes—the Colonies, situated agreeably by the port; it is also a hotel and has 16 rooms. The chef at present is Henri Martin, ex-chef of Decré at Nantes, who was elected *meilleur ouvrier de l'ouest* in 1958, and is creator of the *canard au Muscadet* which had the *Médaille d'Or* at Nantes in 1962. During the Christmas week of 1962 the Colonies was doing a £1 meal consisting of a dozen oysters, *rouget grillé* (or *filet de sole*), game or a grill, salad, cheese, and fruit or *bûche de Noël*—excellent value—and in addition serving a cheap meal getting the *Guide Michelin*'s mark for good value.

But when I go and stay in the Morbihan to see the Carnac megaliths I do not stay in Carnac itself—Ville or Plage—or in Auray or Vannes, but at La Trinité-sur-Mer, a small village which is half fishing port and half the home of yachtsmen living in various parts of north-western France. I have known it for over a quarter of a century. It would be idle nostalgic clap-trap to say that I remember it as an unspoilt Breton village and that it is no different these days. It is different. The Hôtel des Voyageurs has built an extension with 25 rooms and a new dining-room; a new hotel with a fine view was being built when I was last there in the Christmas of 1962. The French Government is spending a lot of money on anchorages and facilities for yachting so that the place can cope with all varieties of *sports nautiques*. I am told that in the height of the season the village street is packed with cars and visitors. So it should be. I go in the off season, but the prosperity it deserves will not kill its village nature, and I know that when I drive over the bridge and see the harbour and the boats before me it will only be a few minutes before I bring my car to a halt outside the Hôtel des Voyageurs, and walk into the bar and order a glass of

A view of La-Trinité-sur-mer

Muscadet. Will Madame Le Rouzic still be there playing *belotte* in the corner? She is, and all is well with the world. I can walk next door to buy the papers from the newspaper boy with the limp, and walk on down the street past the butcher, and the *charcuterie*, and the shop selling everything for ships, and the *épicerie*, and the two cafés, and down to the end of the harbour and stand by the notice telling me not to climb up on to the harbour beacon and look out into the Atlantic. I find, and I know it is subjective and emotional, a peace passing all understanding on occasions like this. That is why, and I confess it at once, southern Brittany now means to me not only megaliths, but La Trinité.

But to readers of this book it means, where to stay? There are three hotels (plus the fourth in process of construction 1962–3). They are the Hôtel des Voyageurs on the quay, and the Hôtel de Commerce (a *routier* establishment) and the Hôtel de L'Etoile de L'Océan on the Locmariaquer-Carnac road at the head of the harbour. I have never stayed in the Commerce or

A view of La-Trinité-sur-mer

the Etoile de L'Océan, but have studied their menus with care; each advertises meals from 6 francs upwards and the 6 franc meal was in both places a four-course affair with shellfish hors-d'oeuvre, fish, a meat course and cheese or fruit. These would be the places for people to stay who are on a tight budget: not that the Voyageurs is expensive. Its *pension* figures in 1962 were 35 to 40 s.t.c. as compared with 25 to 30 at the Etoile and 18 to 25 at the Commerce. Madame Le Rouzic's gastronomic meal at the Voyageurs is fantastic value; a first course which is a *dégustation de fruits de mer*, then an enormous *sole meunière*, a third course of steak or *côte d'agneau* or chicken, cheese and dessert—all for eighteen francs. It is an astonishing sight to see the *dégustations de fruits de mer* taking place; six dishes arrive each piled high—oysters in one, *palourdes* in another, *bigorneaux* in a third, *langoustines* in a fourth, and then a dish of ordinary crabs and of *étrilles*. The degustation begins, and about three-quarters of an hour to an hour later the table is mound high with shells, decorticated *langoustines* and cracked claws. The *menu gastronomique* is something to be attempted at the Voyageurs only once in a while; the ordinary *pension* meals are splendid. I say

Lady eating crab at Locmariaquer

ordinary but they are far from ordinary—and anything you want, within reason, will be specially done for you. The fish market is just across the road from the Voyageurs and you can indicate what fish you want to eat. It is all a tremendous education in the identification of crustaceans and fish and in the pleasure of eating them. It is only if you are one of those sad people who cannot eat shellfish that you are likely to find eating in Brittany dull. I must confess that I am not a great eater of *bigorneaux* (winkles) nor of uncooked *palourdes* and *praires*, but could there be a more lovely meal than a dozen *belons*, followed by a dozen *palourdes farcies*, and a *sole meunière*, with a bottle of Muscadet and the view across the harbour?

It is often said that there are no good cooks in Brittany, that the country cooks itself, that with its incomparable shellfish, its *pré-salé* mutton, and ducks there is nothing to do. But this is not true.

134

✤ IX ✤

The Carnac Megaliths

Let us leave St-Cornély and the bathing-beaches of Carnac-Plage, the delights of the Miln-Le Rouzic Museum, and the oysters and Muscadet *chez* Madame Le Rouzic at La Trinité, and set out to see what we are here to see, the megalithic antiquities of the countryside. Immediately there are three things calling out to be seen first: the great alignments, the Tumulus de St-Michel and the Tumulus de Kercado.

We begin, of course, with the alignments. To get to them we leave the church behind us and go north. There are signposts pointing to the Alignements de Menec; and in just under a mile you will discover yourself, as literal translations of French guidebooks so delightfully say, in the middle of the Menec alignments. Augustus Hare has described his arrival at the Carnac alignments in the late nineteenth century: 'A wild and beautiful spot', he wrote. 'The stones, which are of a delicate grey-green colour, rise like an army, in battalions, from the heather.' The folk tale has it that the alignments are in fact soldiers who pursued St-Cornély, but were turned into stone; so others had the same idea as Augustus Hare before him.

On the way out to the alignments you will pass the Dolmen de Cruz Moquen; it is a free-standing structure with a cross on top of it. At first the Christian Church was opposed to megaliths as survivals of paganism, and then, later, with graceful compromise, arranged for them to be Christianized. Several menhirs in Brittany have crosses on top of them; in one place in north Brittany and in another in north Spain near Oviedo megalithic tombs are incorporated in modern churches. The Tumulus de St-Michel has a Christian chapel on top of it. (Plate 16).

The main Carnac alignments extend for a distance of several miles and comprise in all several thousands of stones.

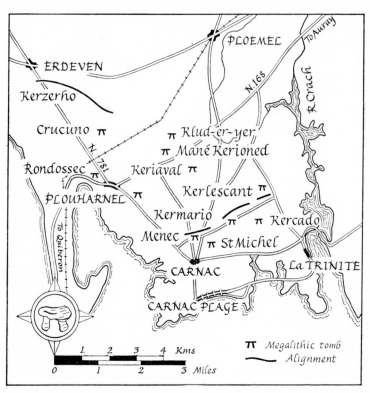

Map 5.   The main Carnac Megalithic sites

They fall into three distinct groups that are referred to as the alignments of Menec, Kermario and Kerlescant. We begin with Menec, and one of the main roads from Carnac cuts right through the centre of the Menec alignments. The Menec series is 1,167 metres long; its average width is 100 metres. It consists of 1,169 single standing stones arranged as follows: 1,099 in the eleven rows and seventy in the cromlech

at the west end of the lines.[1] The general orientation of these
lines is east by north-east. The cromlech is half on one side of
the general line of the alignments. The highest stone in the
Menec series is 4 metres, the smallest only 60 centimetres high.
You will find many other stones around which may be parts of
other menhirs or displaced menhirs. The cromlech itself at the
east end partly surrounds and is partly incorporated in the little
hamlet of Menec. A good view of the Menec alignments is provided by the air photograph (Plate 15) taken before the post-
war rearrangements. There now exists a good motor road running
the whole length of the alignments. You can turn off halfway
along the road from Plouharnel to Carnac, and drive along the
south side of the alignments all the way until you hit the main
road from Auray to La Trinité-sur-Mer.

From the east end of the Menec alignments to the beginning
of the Kermario alignments is 340 metres. The Kermario group
is 1,120 metres long, with an average width of 101 metres. It
contains 982 menhirs placed in ten lines ranging from north-
east to south-west. The largest is 6½ metres and the smallest
about 50 centimetres. There is at the present day no trace of a
cromlech at the south-west end, but most people think that one
did exist there. There are three additional features to be
observed in the Kermario alignments: first, in the middle of
them, in front of the farm of La Petite-Métairie, are three menhirs at right angles to the main line, as though marking a fresh
line to the south; second, to the south of the alignments is a
small, but characteristic, free-standing burial chamber; and,
thirdly, at the east end of the alignments, where they are often
referred to as the Manio section of the Kermario alignments,
they pass over what we should call in southern Britain an
unchambered long barrow and which is referred to in French as
a *tertre tumulaire* or a *tertre allongé*. This site was excavated in
1922; it was roughly rectangular, and had in it a large menhir
higher than most around it, and not with the same orientation

---

[1] All these figures are taken from Le Rouzic's guide-book already mentioned, and it seemed better to keep them in the original metric measure-
ments.

as the other menhirs in the alignments. At its base were carved five zigzag lines which are generally interpreted as serpents. I know that the interpretation of megalithic art is a matter of much discussion and uncertainty, but these five zigzag lines do look like serpents. They can be inspected at present on the site; the menhir stands up conspicuously above the neighbouring ones, and an iron gate leads down into a small room in which the decorated base of the menhir is clearly seen.[1] Near these engraved serpents were found during the 1922 excavations five small polished stone axes in the ground with their cutting edges sticking up in the air. Like the unchambered long barrows of southern Britain, long funerary mounds without any stone burial chambers in them, this Manio monument probably belongs to the first half of the third millennium B.C., and its relationship to the alignments gives us some clue, however slight, to the date of the alignments.[2]

The alignments are broken again for nearly 400 metres between the east end of the Kermario group and the south-west end of the Kerlescant group. The Kerlescant group is 880 metres long and 139 metres wide, and the lines are broken for 200 metres behind the village. In the village itself you can see a great number of menhirs. At the west end is a square cromlech with rounded corners—it is just as well we are using the Breton word 'cromlech', because one could not intelligibly speak of a square stone-circle—and at its northern side is a long mound with a menhir 4 feet high at its western end. It is another *tertre tumulaire* or unchambered long barrow, like the one we have just been describing at Kermario. The Kerlescant alignments themselves comprise 579 menhirs of which thirty-nine are in the cromlech and 540 in the thirteen parallel lines. To the north of the alignments is a long mound with a closed megalithic burial chamber in it which was excavated in the nineteenth century by the Rev. W. C. Lukis.

[1] Perhaps I should have said long ere this moment in this book that a good torch or a supply of candles and matches are essential for dolmen and cave art hunting, except in those monuments that are well lit, such as Lascaux.

[2] For a full discussion of these unchambered long barrows see S. Piggott, *Neolithic Cultures of the British Isles* (1954).

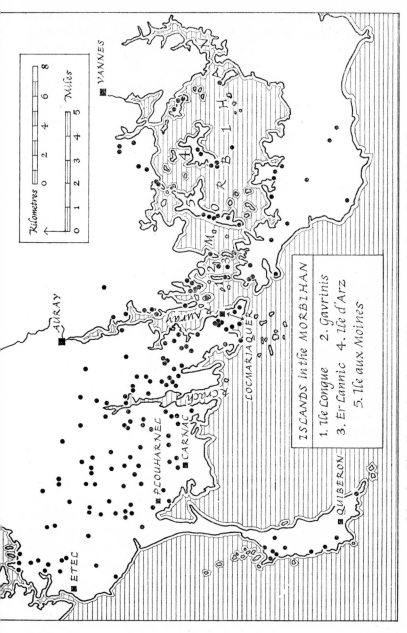

Map 6. *The distribution of megalithic monuments in the south of the Morbihan*

It is surprising that we have got so far in these chapters on Carnac without mentioning this splendid man, who wrote so much on megalithic monuments in the nineteenth century and did so much to interest a wide public in these prehistoric monuments. In 1875 he published *A Guide to the Principal Chambered Barrows and Other Prehistoric Monuments, etc., of South Brittany.* He had spent seven summers, as he said, 'in making myself acquainted with all the principal monuments', and his *Guide*, though, of course out of print, is still very valuable. In a way, although confined to the Breton megaliths, his intentions in writing his book eighty years ago were the same as those which have prompted me to write this book, but he is more scathing in his criticism of the hasty traveller than I should be.

> It was always a source of deep regret to me [he wrote] to observe the hasty step with which archaeological tourists passed over the country, as though their great object was to see as many monuments as possible in one day, and not to study and learn. To this reprehensible precipitancy may be attributed the sadly defective knowledge which is conspicuous in many professing antiquaries both at home and abroad on the subject of chambered barrows. ... If the Traveller desires to learn something from his visit to this wonderful district he should devote to it not less than a week, bearing in mind the French proverb: '*Qui trop embrasse mal étreint.*'

Let us return to the chambered barrow which Lukis excavated, and which stands to the north of the Kerlescant alignments. It was excavated about 1848 'in a careless and partial manner', says Lukis sharply. He then re-excavated it in 1868,[1] and showed it to be a long barrow 150 feet in length containing a long narrow chamber, 54 feet by 5 feet, divided into two nearly equal compartments by two upright stones. On the adjacent edges of the two upright stones semicircular hollows

---

[1] His account of his excavations is to be found in the *Journal of the British Archaeological Association*, 1868, pp. 40ff., and a brief account also in his *Guide*, p. 18.

are cut, forming what is known as a 'porthole': a second port-hole existed on the south side of the chamber. These porthole devices are a standard feature in the architecture of some megalithic tombs: many exist in megalithic tombs in southern Spain and in rock-cut tombs near Lisbon, and there are good examples of portholes in south France and in the Paris Basin. In Brittany, the porthole device is rare, and this makes this Kerlescant tomb particularly interesting. The Tolven and the Men-an-tol in Cornwall, which we have already mentioned, have been claimed as portholes. Portholes certainly exist in the Cotswold megalithic tombs, such as Rodmarton and Avening. W. C. Lukis's excavations in this monument yielded pottery, undecorated round-bottomed ware and also beakers, three flint arrow-heads, a pendant of rock crystal, a second pendant of clay-slate, several flint scrapers and flakes and a beautiful polished axe of fibrolite. All these objects are now in the British Museum.

We have left the subject of alignments for a moment while we have become interested in the Kerlescant tomb. There is another tomb nearby that we should visit; this is the monument of Kercado, which you will find south-east of the eastern end of the Kermario alignments. It is a fine circular barrow about 100 feet in diameter and 10 feet high. This barrow covers and contains a splendid megalithic tomb consisting of a passage leading into a rectangular chamber. A few of the stones at Kercado are decorated; the most obvious and interesting design is on the underside of the capstone and looks like a hafted axe. This tomb was excavated in 1863 by René Galles and Lefebvre, and again in 1924 by Le Rouzic in making some reconstruction and conservation work. The earlier excavators found axe-heads of diorite and jadeite, pendants of serpentine and schist, arrowheads, beads of callais, pottery and fragments of human bones, while the Le Rouzic excavations yielded a very considerable quantity of pottery, including beaker pottery again, three arrowheads, two gold plaques and no less than 147 beads of callais. The finds from the earlier excavations may be seen at Vannes in the Museum of the local archaeological society, the

Société Polymathique du Morbihan; Le Rouzic's finds are in the Carnac Museum.[1]

These finds have been listed because they give us a good idea of the sort of things buried with the dead in these great tombs. Kercado is a splendid example of the classic megalithic construction of walling stones, dry walling and capstones. It is also a classic example of a passage grave. It is, of course, not to be expected that all the thousands of megalithic tombs in western Europe should have been constructed in the same way or to the same plan. Indeed, there is such a wide variety of plan that archaeologists sometimes spend an inordinate amount of time in devising and disputing suitable morphological classifications of these tombs. We have already seen that one kind of monument is the single chamber, either rectangular or round or polygonal. Two other main forms are the passage-grave (called in France the *dolmen à galerie*) of which Kercado is a very good example, and the gallery grave (called in France the *allée couverte*) of which Kerlescant is a good example (Figs. 10, 11, 12). The passage grave has a passage leading into a chamber, whereas the gallery grave is itself a long tomb without any obvious morphological widening into a chamber. Good examples of passage and gallery graves are given in Fig. 10. The distinction between these two types must not be regarded as anything fundamental; they are differences in styles of funerary architecture, perhaps reflecting different communities or traditions. And both forms almost certainly derive from the same basic traditions in the west Mediterranean and, ultimately, the east Mediterranean.

This is not the place to discuss in detail the origins and spread of megalithic tombs. Their distribution in Europe is shown on Map 10. Many different theories exist about their origins, but that most widely held at the present day is that they represent the tombs of settlers and prospectors who spread from the east and middle Mediterranean to the west Mediterranean, and then through western Europe by two routes, the Atlantic

---

[1] The 1863 excavations are described in the *Bulletin de la Société Polymathique* for that year, and Le Rouzic's in that journal for 1927. The 1863 finds are in the *Catalogue* of the Vannes Museum (1921), H, 610–35.

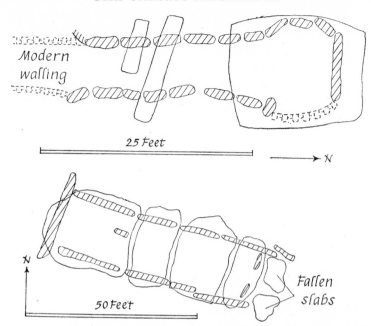

Fig. 10. *Plans to illustrate the two main types of French megalithic tomb:* Top, *a Passage Grave* (or Dolmen à Galerie), *and Bottom, a Gallery Grave* (or Allée Couverte)

route from Iberia and the cross-French routes from the Languedoc. It is possible that the Carnac area received influences from both areas; it was certainly the main settlement area of the megalithic tomb builders who came by sea from Iberia—a sort of prehistoric metropolis. These great stone tombs that we visit in and around Carnac should then be envisaged as the tombs of these early settlers in the third millennium B.C.

Why did this movement of people occur along the western seaways? Were the builders of these tombs looking for somewhere to live, or were they looking for raw materials needed in their Mediterranean homes? It seems most likely that they were concerned, among other things, with the exploitation of the copper and tin resources of Ireland, Britain and Brittany. The development of metal-working for the first time in western Europe seems to coincide in time with the spread of these tombs.

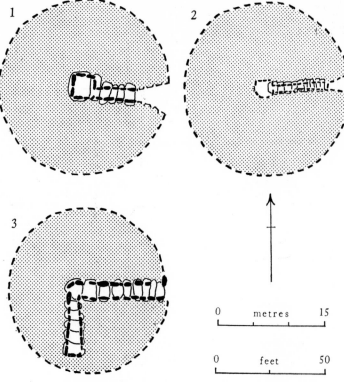

Fig. 11. *Breton Passage Graves: 1. Kercado; 2. Ile Longue;*
3. Le Bono, Plougoumelen

Yet the number of such tombs in north-western Europe with
any copper tools in them is almost negligible. Why was this?
Perhaps because all the metal was for export to the Mediterranean, or because there was some sacred *tabu*? Fine polished
axes of stone are put in these great tombs; some of them are
extremely thin, could never have been used, and are green in
colour as though imitating metal. That is one of the two minor
mysteries of the megalith builders in the Carnac region. The
other is where they lived. This is a general problem in relation
to megalith builders in north-western Europe as a whole, and
it is strange that those who spent so long on building their
tombs should spend such a little time on their houses and

20. (a) One of the three chambers at Mané-Kerioned

20. (b) Christianized burial chamber at Carnac

21. The sculptured stone in Mané-er-Hroeck, Locmariaquer

villages. One or two village sites in the Carnac neighbourhood dating from this period exist—the Camp de Lizo is one, and well repays a climb up to see it. It is constructed on the hillside overlooking the river Crach and is the sort of place where settlers coming to Brittany from the south might well have landed and made their headquarters. The banks and ditches of this settlement are not difficult to find except that they and a part of the interior of the site are covered by gorse, bramble and bracken; if you resolutely tear yourself through all this you will

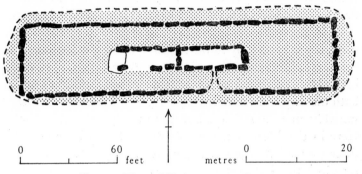

0   60   feet   metres   0   20

Fig. 12. *Plan of Kerlescant near Carnac*

see a settlement site of the megalith builders. There is also a small V-shaped passage grave in a round mound inside the ramparts. It is curious that we do not know more of where the megalith builders lived—perhaps their settlement sites lie under the present villages of Carnac, Plouharnel and La Trinité.

Another question: What about the alignments, and what relation do they bear to the constructors of the tombs? The real truth is that the great alignments of the Morbihan, like the great stone circles of Britain, are something special developed in those separate regions. There is nothing like Stonehenge and Avebury outside Great Britain, and nothing really to compare with the Carnac alignments outside the Morbihan. These alignments are a *tour de force*, probably architecturally and religiously, within the early communities who built these collective tombs. We cannot date the alignments with great certainty. We have seen that the Kermario alignments in the field of Menec pass over and are therefore later than what is probably a kind of unchambered long barrow of the early third millennium B.C. James Miln was able to show that the alignments were earlier than the Roman villa he excavated and that the villa utilized some of the broken menhirs. The alignments are then somewhere between, say, 1800 B.C. and the Roman period. Can we not refine the dates within this very broad bracket? I think we can, and the strong probability is that the alignments date within the great *floruit* of megalithic cultures in southern Britain—somewhere between 3000 and 1500 B.C.

Walk along the whole length of these great alignments again; walk, if you can, early in the morning or on a moonlit evening. It is a most impressive experience, and one which, like standing in the Upper Palaeolithic decorated caves of southern France, is both moving and tantalizing: we see the form of what was presumably an early religion, but we can only guess at its content. Here in the Morbihan the guesses must be wilder even than those we made in the Dordogne caves. Do you see figures moving along the long avenues of stone to some sacred rituals in the cromlechs at the west end? So do I, but they are so shadowy that they vanish as I get nearer. The rituals and beliefs of the prehistoric past lie buried, and only the imperishable treasures of stone and gold in the tombs survive, and the tall grey stones to beg the question and mock in silence at our inability to answer.

Looking to seaward from any point along the alignments you see to the east of the little township of Carnac a long, flat-topped hill. This is the Tumulus de St-Michel, and is the third site that must be visited, after the alignments and Kercado. A by-road leads up to it from near the Museum; you pass the hotel, and at the back is the entrance to the tomb. A guide will take you round, having first equipped you with candles and warned you to beware of knocking your head against the roof. As you wait to go in, little boys from the village will surround you begging to be allowed to recite what they call 'the legend of the tomb'. It is a modern poem of calypso type, recounting, with some accuracy, the history of the monuments in the neigh-

bourhood of Carnac and how modern excavations have super-
seded the guesses of earlier antiquaries. It is not long, and well
repays the few coins you will give the boys.

This monument has a Chapel of St-Michel on top of it; you
should certainly climb to the top (Plate 16). From it on a good
day there is a most excellent view of the countryside and out to
sea, and a *table d'orientation* enables you to identify the main
points. The Tumulus de St-Michel is another long barrow: a
very long barrow—indeed, one of the longest chambered
barrows in Europe. It is about 370 to 380 feet in length, nearly
200 feet broad, and is 32 to 35 feet high. It was first excavated
by René Galles in 1862, and then again by Zacharie Le Rouzic
in the period 1900–6.

When you have walked along the alignments and seen Kercado and the Tumulus de St-Michel, you have indeed seen a
very good selection of the megalithic monuments in the neighbourhood of Carnac. There are, of course, many more to see,
and by using the Le Rouzic *Guide* you can plan more walks and
drives to take in more of these remarkable monuments. I will
suggest here only one further expedition in the Carnac area. Go
along the road to Plouharnel, where the main Auray-Quiberon
road (and railway) cuts across the Carnac-Etel road. On your
way and just before getting to Plouharnel you will see a small
dolmen in the hedge on the right of the road. It is a good
example of a single chamber and shows the difficulty of arguing
from such monuments. With the road cutting across it, we can
probably never know whether it originally had a passage and
whether the apparently simple chamber was no more than the
remains of a more complicated plan. This particular monument
has a special place in my memory because when I was in India
at the end of the 1939–45 War it suddenly appeared on a news-
reel. Quiberon was one of the pockets of German resistance
after France was liberated, and fighting went on late in the
Carnac-Plouharnel neighbourhood. At one time the line of
battle was across this very road: it was a strange thing to see,
on the screen thousands of miles away in India, soldiers with
machine guns firing out of this dolmen.

When you meet the main road, turn right and proceed for a few miles along the Route Nationale to Auray. Soon on your left and immediately on the side of the road you will come to the Mané Kerioned site (Plate 20, bottom). This is a long, oval or quadrilateral mound which contains three dolmens; they are in shape the sort of monument that causes dispute between archaeologists as to whether to classify them as passage graves or gallery graves. The general plan is bottle-shaped or V-shaped, the two sides splaying out from the entrance to a wide chamber, but the chamber is not sharply demarcated from the passage. They are probably a variant form of the passage grave, and this form, but done on a small scale and called an entrance grave, is found in west Cornwall, the Isles of Scilly and in County Waterford in Ireland. One of the three chambers has decorated designs on eight of its supports. It was excavated first in 1866, and the pottery, flints and polished axes are on view in the Vannes Museum.[1] When Zacharie Le Rouzic was engaged in restoration work at this site in 1922 he found, in the body of the mound, a small stone with two hafted stone axes engraved on it; this original stone is now on view in the Carnac Museum.

When you have studied the splendid monument of Mané Kerioned, walk up the main road towards Auray, and then when the field-hedges give way to a characteristic stretch of *landes* country with pine trees you will see, away to the right, another impressive megalithic tomb, Keriaval (Fig. 13), an oval barrow over 100 feet long with a maximum breadth of 65 to 70 feet, with a fine chamber at the east end. The chamber consists of a double parallel-sided row of walling stones with two side chambers on the north side and the remains of two other side chambers on the south. The site has been dug on various occasions, starting with 1854. It is its plan which is of special interest to visitors from England and Wales; this same plan is shown by several other megalithic monuments in the Morbihan, and one, Klud-er-Yer, is not far from Keriaval, on the other side of the main road. This plan, which for convenience of

[1] *Bulletin de la Société Polymathique du Morbihan*, 1866, p. 94; *Catalogue du Musée archéologique de Vannes*, 1921, p. 19.

reference I have called a transepted gallery grave, is very like the plan of some megalithic monuments in south-east Wales (such as Parc-le-Breos Cwm in the Gower Peninsula) and the Cotswolds (such as Notgrove, Nympsfield and the famous Hetty Pegler's Tump or Uley Barrow), and it seems to many archaeologists very probable that the megalithic monuments of

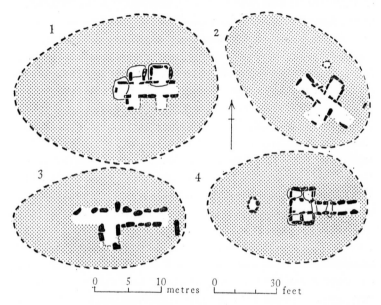

Fig. 13. Transepted Gallery Graves in Brittany: 1. Keriaval; 2. Herbignac; 3. Grah Niol; 4. Mané Groh, Erdeven

what are called the Cotswold-Severn group are to be derived from monuments like Keriaval and Klud-er-Yer. This means that we envisage early in the first half of the third millennium B.C. a movement of people from the Morbihan and the Loire Atlantique up the Bristol Channel. These early Armoricans colonized south Wales and the Cotswolds and Mendips and built tombs of various types, including this transepted gallery grave. Some have argued that this name is a misnomer and that the monuments are really variants of passage graves. That dispute does not concern us here; both passage graves and gallery graves occur in the Morbihan, and one can argue a possible derivation either way.

What is important to realize is that this specialized plan of tomb, the transepted gallery grave, has a very restricted distribution, and that it is really confined to north-western France and the Severn-Cotswold area. The distribution of monuments of this type is shown on Map 7. Recently in the British Isles very important excavations have been made in three of our transepted gallery graves, namely West Kennet in Wiltshire, Parc-le-Breos Cwm in Glamorganshire, and Wayland's Smithy in Berkshire.[1] What we now want is modern excavation in one or two of the comparable monuments in Brittany.

Returning to Plouharnel, turn right along the road to Etel. There is much of interest to see along this road. First, between the main road and level-crossing there is, to the south of the road, the remarkable site of Rondossec, another barrow with three large dolmens in it. Further on along the road to Etel and Belz, you can turn off to the right and visit a group of megalithic monuments, of which the most impressive is the dolmen of Crucuno (Plate 18 bottom). This is said to be the largest dolmen in the Morbihan; it is certainly most impressive and photographs well. The capstone is 25 feet long; the whole chamber has an interior height of just over 6 feet, and gives a very good impression of the problems involved in constructing megalithic tombs, and the skills which the megalith builders possessed. Farther along the road westwards the road itself cuts through the alignments of Kerzerho (Plate 15). You then drive through the village of Erdeven, and from here westwards you should visit the very picturesque fishing port of Etel and from there or Belz make a pilgrimage to the Chapel of St-Cado. Cado is one of the many Welsh saints who came to Brittany in the fifth century A.D. to Christianize the Armoricans and to minister to the Britons who were emigrating to Brittany. The Chapel of St-Cado is connected to the mainland by a causeway (Plate 13), and the tradition is that this causeway was built by

---

[1] The excavations at West Kennet have been published in S. Piggott, *The West Kennet Long Barrow: Excavations 1955–6* (London, 1962).

Map 7. *Distribution of transepted Gallery Graves in southern Britain and north-western France*

the Devil in a single night on condition that St-Cado should give to him the soul of the first foot passenger to cross over next morning. At first light next morning St-Cado set his cat to walk across the causeway; the Devil, thwarted, tried to destroy the causeway, and the wily St-Cado, in trying to stop him, slipped on a rock. The place where he slipped, the Glissade de St-Cado, is now surmounted by a Calvary.

Whatever we may think of this story, which I always think reflects more credit on the cat than on St-Cado or the Devil, the chapel and the causeway form a delightful spot at the present day. This is a pleasant place to meditate on the close relations that existed in ancient times between parts of Britain and the south of Brittany; St-Cado, or St. Cadoc, as he is usually known in Wales, came to this district from those very parts of south-east Wales which we have suggested were colonized by the builders of the transepted gallery graves.

The Calvary at St-Cado, Morbihan

✤ X ✤

Locmariaquer, Vannes and the Morbihan

T he traveller who is really interested in these prehistoric megalithic monuments will spend many days in the Carnac area. He must not neglect to move on to Locmariaquer and the islands of the Morbihan. The traveller who can spend only a very short time in the Morbihan must also not neglect to devote at least a day to this country east of Carnac; a day is the minimum time that can be spent, and in that time only the essential and most important monuments can be seen, i.e. half a day for Gavr'innis and Er Lannic, and half a day for the great Locmariaquer monuments. Let us begin with Locmariaquer.

The peninsula of land formed by the River Crach on the west and the River Auray on the east, with its base the main road from Auray to Quiberon, is extremely rich in prehistoric remains. Indeed, it is the area *par excellence* for seeing the great megalithic tombs, just as the Carnac area, although it, too, is so rich in megalithic tombs, is the region *par excellence* for visiting the great stone rows. In this small area of land forming a rectangle about four miles broad by nine miles long are some of the most famous megalithic monuments in the world: the Table des Marchands, the Mané Ruthual, the Mané Lud and the Mané-er-Hroeck among chambered tombs, and the Grand Menhir Brisé, one of the most curious of all remains from prehistoric Europe. The whole area can easily be visited in a day, or the most important monuments in half a day, from Vannes, Auray,

Carnac or Quiberon. The little town of Crach lies inland at the centre of the rectangle, the village of St-Philibert at the south-west corner, and Locmariaquer at the south-east corner. The bridge across the Crach at La Trinité, which was destroyed in 1944, has now happily been rebuilt, which will save you the

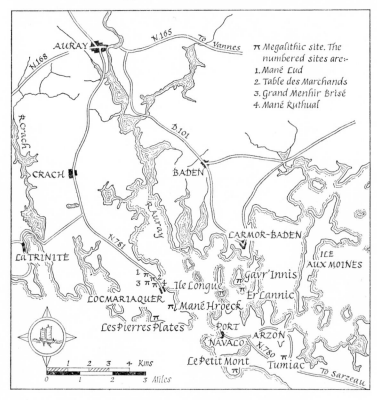

Map 8. Locmariaquer and the Gulf of Morbihan

detour up to the Quiberon-Auray road that I have many times had to make in recent years.

There are two main groups of prehistoric sites worth concentrating on: those between Crach and the river, and the ones between the Crach-St-Philibert-Locmariaquer road junction and Locmariaquer itself. These latter are the famous sites and demand our prior attention. As you come down the road from this junction towards Locmariaquer you will first observe two single-chamber dolmens—one on the right of the road, the other on the left. That on the right is Kercadoret; that on the left is Kerveresse. Kerveresse has a large capstone, the underside of which is covered with cup-marks, and some of these are so made that they must have been constructed before the capstone was placed in position. Three of the walling stones of the chamber are decorated with engraved designs; the designs are very faint, but include the ship and crook symbols found commonly in Breton megalithic art. The motifs in Breton art are difficult to describe without giving them some descriptive names; the names I am using here, like ship and crook, are for convenience of description only, and what I mean by them can be seen with reference to the diagram (Fig. 14, p. 158).

Passing on to Locmariaquer, you soon come to the first of the great megalithic tombs: Mané Lud—and the name means only 'hill of ashes'. Immediately as you enter the village this long barrow lies to the right of the road and at right angles to it. It is 260 feet in length by 160 feet wide and 16 to 17 feet high. Climb on to the top of it, and on a fine day you will see to the east of you the waters of the Golfe du Morbihan, the landscape studded with trees and islands. The great barrow extends from east to west; it has at its west end, not actually opening from the west end, but from the south edge close to the west end, an extremely fine passage grave. The west end of the barrow abuts on to and is incorporated in farm buildings and a farmyard, and you squeeze your way into the passage past the walls of a cowshed.

The passage grave consists of a passage lined by thirteen orthostats leading into a roughly rectangular chamber. Four capstones remain roofing the passage, and an enormous capstone roofs the chamber and extends to the north of it; this capstone, which is at the present day broken into two pieces, measures 28 feet in length and 16 feet in extreme breadth. Eight of the orthostats walling the passage and chamber of Mané Lud have been described as decorated, but I am not happy about the alleged decorations on some of them. The stone at the back of the chamber facing you as you walk in down the passage has, to my mind, a very doubtful design,[1] but there is no doubt about the engraved symbols on the stones on each side of this end slab: to the right is a cornerstone with the yoke symbols,[2] and next to it a stone with more yoke symbols, axe symbols and a sun symbol. On the left of the end stone as you face it is a stone with axe, crook and yoke symbols and possibly an eyebrow motif. The three decorated stones in the passage call for special notice; the third stone on the left as you walk up the passage from the entrance has clear yoke symbols and a big ship symbol; the fifth stone on the left has at least twelve yoke symbols, while the last stone on the right before entering the chamber is clearly marked with yoke, ship and buckle patterns.

Mané Lud was excavated in 1863–64 by René Galles, who cut a wide trench along the length of the mound. He discovered at the east end a slightly curved wall of small juxtaposed menhirs, upon five of which, at intervals, were horses' skulls. In the centre of the barrow Galles found a small closed burial chamber containing the remains of two individuals, one cremated and one unburnt; this little burial chamber was walled with dry-walling and roofed by corbelling. In it, together with the remains, was an axe of fibrolite, flint flakes and fragments of pottery. The great megalithic chamber had been open for a long time, and nothing was found in it during the 1863—64 excavations except underneath a flooring stone at the entrance of the chamber. When this was lifted, a small hole was discovered, and in this was a pottery spindle-whorl, two flint flakes, a bead of jasper, charcoal and more pottery. In 1911 Zacharie Le Rouzic re-excavated the site and discovered five gold bands, flint arrowheads, two dozen beads, a pendant of callais and some more pottery, including beaker.[3]

---

[1] Le Rouzic's drawing in the *Corpus des Signes Gravés*, Plate 47, seems only to record natural breaks in the rock surface.

[2] This stone has three small holes which are the result of modern fastenings.

[3] René Galles' finds are in the Musée at Vannes (*Catalogue*, 1921, p. 42), and the account of his excavations in the *Bulletin de la Société Polymathique du Morbihan*, for 1864; Le Rouzic's finds are at Carnac and his published account in the 1911 volume of the *Bulletin*.

From the top of the chamber at Mané Lud look south and you will see the Table des Marchands and the Grand Menhir Brisé. You can walk to them along a path direct, or you can go along the main road past the cemetery until you meet a sign-post pointing westwards to these sites. If you walk directly from the Mané Lud your path will skirt the eastern side of a ruined long barrow. This barrow has had much of its material carted away, but sufficient remains to estimate its original dimensions as over 400 feet in length and 200 in breadth. In the centre—a little path leads through the gorse bushes to it—is a small burial chamber partly dry-walled and partly walled by orthostats.

The Table des Marchands is a particularly magnificent example of a megalithic passage grave, and its proportions show up well in the photograph (Plate 18, top). It does not, however, look like this at the present day, because it has been restored, re-walled and a mound built over it. There were originally traces of a circular mound 130 feet in diameter, and Lukis in his *Guide* in 1875 described it as 'still partially buried in a circular mound'. The passage leads in from the south side to a large, approximately circular chamber roofed by a huge capstone 20 feet long by 13 feet wide. On the underside of the capstone are, deeply engraved, some designs which certainly include a hafted axe and some crook symbols. The endstone of the chamber is one of the most famous examples of Breton mega-lithic art; it is decorated in relief with rows of crook symbols framed in what looks like a large buckler symbol; there are four rows of crooks and a sun symbol in the middle. The buckler symbol is fringed with curving lines. Some of the megalithic art is difficult to see, but this art at Table des Marchands is not. The most casual visitor to the site sees these designs clearly. But as one looks at this splendidly decorated stone one is most violently filled with the despair that must come to all prehistoric archaeologists. What do these designs mean? Why were they made? Unfortunately, there is no certain answer. We can only guess, and we will postpone our guess until we have seen other decorated sites in the Morbihan.

Acording to Lukis, 'human bones and charcoal, fragments of

Fig. 14. *Some of the characteristic symbols represented in south Breton megalithic art: 1. The* yoke *symbol. 2. Concentric half-ellipses. 3. Hafted axe. 4. The* crook *motif. 5. The* ship *symbol. 6. Axehead. 7. Bow. 8. Rayed circle or* sun *symbol. 9. Zigzag lines or snakes? 10. The* buckler *motif. 11. Stylized human figure?*

clay vessels, and a flint axe were found here' in 1811. In the Museum at Vannes there is a fibrolite axe, a fragment of a diorite axe, a flint arrowhead and pottery from the site. This remarkable monument was restored, following its acquisition by the State, in 1883 and 1905. In 1922, while Zacharie Le Rouzic was engaged in further reconstruction and repair work, he thought he found on the north side of the endstone some more designs which, according to him, included an oculi or eye motif. I am not in my own mind happy that these designs exist, but visitors seeing this stone in a variety of lighting conditions may be able to confirm or deny these reputed designs.[1]

Not far from the great Table des Marchands is the Grand Menhir Brisé. What the visitor sees today are four great pieces of stone which were once a single enormous menhir; when intact, this measured 67 feet 6 inches in length by 13 feet 6 inches in width by 7 feet 6 inches thick (Plate 18, bottom). The height of Cleopatra's Needle on the Thames Embankment is 68 feet 6 inches, and its weight is 180 tons. The Grand Menhir Brisé is much larger and thicker, and its weight is computed as about 330 tons. It is widely held that this great menhir was struck by lightning and broken into four parts; others believe that its present state is merely the result of an ordinary fall; yet others believe that it was thrown down following the Council of Nantes edicts against worshipping stones. The problem is still unsolved, and there are some who—I think perversely—believe the four pieces were never part of a single menhir. I think they were, and that their shaping leaves no other conclusion possible, although how the great menhir was broken is certainly not known. What is known is that it was in its present condition at least by A.D. 1727. If you pause for a moment before you leave this group of monuments at Locmariaquer and think of the amazing structures within one single glance—the great long barrow of Mané Lud, the other ruined long barrow, the Table des Marchands, and the 330-ton Grand Menhir originally standing dominating the scene to a height of well over 60 feet—you cannot but get a very astonishing impression

---

[1] On the Table des Marchands see *Bulletin de la Société Polymathique du Morbihan*, for 1890, and Z. Le Rouzic and Ch. Keller, *La Table des Marchands, ses signes sculptés* (Nancy, 1910) and the *Corpus des Signes Gravés*, p. 122 and Plates 38–43.

of the crafts and the religious convictions of the early Breton megalith builders.

Moving on into Locmariaquer, you come to the large burial chamber known as Mané Ruthual or Bé-er-Groah. If you like to follow the main road into the town, you will find, by the Mairie, a small footpath marked with the name of this site. It may lead you into a garden, an allotment or a backyard, but with good luck and judgment—and if you have been pursuing all the megaliths described in the last chapter and this, you will be getting by now a bump of megalithic topography—you may arrive at this site, another very large and most impressive megalithic tomb. No trace of its mound survives at present. All you see is a long passage leading up to a roughly circular chamber. The coverstone of the chamber is a truly gigantic stone 27 feet long by 14 feet 6 inches wide. It was, until recently, broken into two parts, and the larger part rested on the ground to the back of the chamber. It has now been lifted up and propped on newly made walls which gives a very curious impression of an additional chamber behind the main one. Engraved designs have been recognized and described in this monument—on the underside of the great capstone and on the underside of the capstone roofing the passage nearest to the chamber itself, and on two or three of the orthostats of the passage. These designs include crook symbols, a buckler symbol and a hafted axe. This monument was partly excavated in 1860 and again in 1865. Finds from Mané Ruthual in the Vannes Museum include flint flakes, a piece of a diorite axe, a spindle-whorl, as well as remains of Roman pottery and statuary and Roman coins[1] (Fig. 15).

From the Mané Ruthual retrace your steps to the Mairie, and you are now in the centre of Locmariaquer. It has a pleasant quayside and port, and if you have already seen enough megalithic monuments you can spend a very happy afternoon sipping drinks and looking out over the waters of the Golfe du Morbihan. There are, however, more important things to do. Two

---

[1] See the Vannes Museum *Catalogue*, 1921, p. 25, and the 1860 and 1885 volumes of the *Bulletin de la Société Polymathique de Morbihan*.

2. The Christianized Menhir of St-Duzec, Côtes-du-Nord

23. (a) Two of the burial chambers at Barnenez South, Côtes-du-Nord

23. (b) Inside the great Gallery Grave of Bagneux, near Saumur, Maine-et-Loire

roads lead on towards the south from Locmariaquer: the first directly south to Kerpenhir; the second south-west—you will find a signpost to it in the middle of the village saying, abruptly, 'Plage: *dolmens*'. We must in turn take both of these roads. The first leads us to Mané-er-Hroeck, the second to Les Pierres Plates, and both these important sites should not be missed (Fig. 15).

Mané-er-Hroeck is just to the right of the main Locmaria-quer-Kerpenhir road some three-quarters of a mile south from Locmariaquer itself (Plate 21). A narrow path between two properties leads into this oval mound of stones about 340 feet in length by 180 to 200 feet in breadth, and over 30 feet in height. On the east side of the barrow are two broken menhirs of very considerable length, one 30 feet and the other 25 feet long. The mound was excavated in 1863 by René Galles and the Prefect of the Morbihan. They discovered in the centre a chamber of irregular form about 12 feet 6 inches by 10 feet by 5 feet high; the side walls are dry-walled, while the roof consists of two large capstones. Near the entrance to the chamber they found a slab covered with engraved designs, and this slab has now been set up inside the tomb. No less than 104 axes were found during these excavations. They were made of various precious stones, such as diorite, chloromelanite, jadeite and fibrolite—the largest of these was just over 18 inches long. There were also found an oval ring or disc of jadeite, nine large callais pendants, a necklace of forty-one callais beads, some flint flakes and a small quantity of pottery sherds. No traces of any burials were found.[1]

Les Pierres Plates is the last of the great megalithic tombs in the immediate neighbourhood of Locmariaquer that the archaeological tourist must visit. It lies right on the edge of the sea, looking out southwards. Its name is due to the very flat and rectangular appearance of most of the capstones. It is a long monument, angled in plan, with a chamber at the far end and one off to the left close to the entrance. This particular

[1] The finds were described in the *Bulletin de la Société Polymathique du Morbihan* in 1863, and are in the Vannes Museum (*Catalogue*, p. 44).

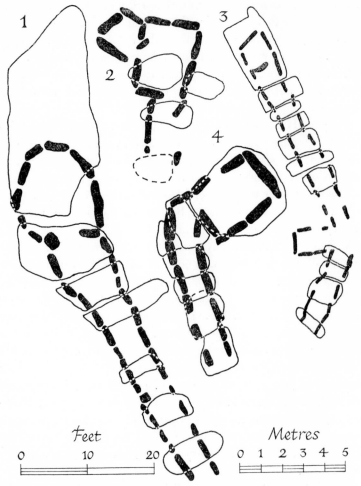

Fig. 15. *Variant Breton Passage Graves: 1. Mané Ruthual. 2. Kermar-*
quer. 3. Les Pierres Plates, Locmariaquer. 4. Kergonfals

form of plan is very interesting: it is one of a small group of what
are often called in French archaeological literature *allées cou-*
vertes coudées; Luffang, near Crach, is another, and Le Rocher,
Plougoumelen, a third. They are probably just specialized local
versions of the basic passage grave plan and need no more
special designation than that of angled passage grave. This

particular monument—Les Pierres Plates—was excavated as long ago as 1811 with no known results, and was restored by the State in 1892. The great interest of the site is its decorated stones. No less than thirteen of the orthostats are decorated, and most of the designs are very clear. They are all of a special kind; the yoke and buckler motifs occur, but the motifs are mainly those shown on the diagram (Fig. 14).

On the way back from Locmariaquer a visit should be paid, if that is possible, to a group of megalithic monuments that lie to the west of Crach, between that village and the River Crach. They include some very good passage graves at Parc Guren and Coed Kerzut and another angled passage grave at Luffang. It was one of the Parc Guren passage graves that yielded the segmented faience bead we have already discussed when visiting the Carnac Museum, and Luffang has designs which are worth comparing with Les Pierres Plates. One of the Luffang designs is reproduced here (Plate 19); it has been interpreted as a stylized octopus.

We must now leave the Crach-Locmariaquer Peninsula and visit the islands of the Morbihan. It used to be possible to hire a boat from Locmariaquer and sail out into the gulf, but now this does not happen, and the only practicable way for the tourist to visit Gavr'innis and Er-Lannic is by the motor-boat service which makes frequent journeys from Larmor-Baden. Larmor-Baden can be reached easily from Auray or Vannes by road, or it can be reached by boat from Vannes. A small steamer service goes from Vannes through the gulf to Locmariaquer and Port Navalo, and calls at Larmor-Baden and other places on the way. I can think of no pleasanter way to see the gulf than in one of these steamers from Vannes; you can, if you organize yourself and study the steamer timetable carefully, have enough time to visit the Ile-aux-Moines and to make a stop long enough at Larmor-Baden to visit Gavr'innis. The Ile-aux-Moines has several megalithic monuments, including the Dolmen de Penhap, a passage grave with three decorated orthostats. The motor-boat service from Larmor-Baden will take you to Gavr'innis, landing you on this island long enough to see the tomb, and will make an additional circuit to Er-Lannic. It used also to be possible to land on the Ile Longue, which has a ruined but still very magnificent corbelled passage grave, but this island is now private property and the site can no longer be visited.

There is no real point in trying to land at Er-Lannic. The essential features of this unusual monument can be seen clearly from the boat. It is referred to locally as Les Cromlechs de Er-Lannic and consists of two stone circles set touching each other so that they give a figure-of-eight plan. The southerly circle is completely covered by the sea, while the northerly circle is covered in part; the sight of the menhirs marching into the water (see Plate 18, top) is an impressive reminder of the changes in land- and sea-levels that have taken place since the time of the megalith builders. This site was excavated by Le Rouzic in the period 1923–26, and the results have been published in a book printed in Vannes in 1930 entitled *Les Cromlechs de Er-Lannic*. The finds, which are in the Carnac Museum, include a large amount of pottery, many decorated vase-supports and beakers, flints, polished stone axes and beads.

Gavr'innis has been described as the most remarkable megalithic monument in Western Europe. It is certainly one of those which, like New Grange in Ireland, demand a very special pilgrimage, and at Gavr'innis it is not because of its size or construction or form, but because of its decorated stones. Gavr'innis—the name means Goat Island—is a round mound some 20 feet high covering a megalithic passage grave which was excavated, without any results, in 1832. The passage and chamber consist of twenty-nine orthostats, and no less than twenty-three of these are decorated, and, unlike many of the decorated stones at which we have been looking, these stones are covered with decoration. At Gavr'innis it is not a question of trying to find some obscure piece of decoration on a stone; here as you stand in the tomb you are surrounded by masses of decoration, and the problem is to try to understand what the artist was at and why. All is done by incised and pocked lines. The motifs include zigzags, concentric semicircles, ellipses,

spirals, axes and other curious geometrical patterns. The richness of these designs has to be seen on the spot to be properly
appreciated.

There is no better place than Gavr'innis to pause and think
about the nature of this megalithic art. The tombs themselves
are the tombs of settlers who came from the Mediterranean,
and the art itself is probably Mediterranean in origin, drawing
its inspiration from two contemporary motifs in the East
Mediterranean: the figure of some funerary deity like the earth
mother goddess, and, secondly, the geometrical motif of spirals
and circles. These motifs travelled with the tomb builders as
part of their magico-religious imagery, and we find them first
on idols and other objects deposited with the dead in southern
Iberia and then appearing on the walls of the tombs themselves
in north-west Iberia and in Brittany and Ireland. As the
distance increased from the Mediterranean, these designs
become less and less representational, and the geometrical
element predominates. This is not to say that all the designs
which are to be seen on the Breton megaliths are to be interpreted as stylized versions of a female goddess figure; indeed,
many have interpreted them in countless other ways, seeing in
the designs ships, octopuses, and even the fingerprints of giants.
Like the tectiforms in Upper Palaeolithic art, we cannot explain
most of the megalithic scribings. I think that some of them are
very clearly stylized faces and figures, but that is as far as we can
go. They do not always make sense if you do remember the
Mediterranean heritage of goddess and spirals; but they make
meaningless nonsense if you do not.

From the top of Gavr'innis you can survey the whole of the
south end of the Morbihan, from Locmariaquer to the west to
the Presqu'île de Rhuys on the east. This peninsula is worth a
very special visit. It too is rich in megalithic remains; two tombs
deserve visits, and these can easily be fitted in between steamers
at Port Navalo. The first is Tumiac and the second Le Petit-
Mont. Both are notable landmarks. Tumiac lies to the north of
the road from Arzon to Sarzeau; it is a large, round mound
covering a closed chamber. As you walk along the steep,

bracken-covered path down into the mound you can appreciate, as one does, for example, in the middle of the Tumulus de St-Michel, the enormous labour that has gone to the construction of such mounds in prehistoric times. From the top there is a splendid view, and just over a mile to the west is the great mound of Le Petit-Mont; it is reached by a side road that branches off from the main road just south of the village of Arzon. Le Petit-Mont is an oval mound nearly 200 feet long by 150 feet broad covering over a passage grave. It was excavated in 1865 when an axe-hammer, pottery, flint arrowheads and callais beads were found. These are in the Vannes Museum. The monument was restored by Le Rouzic in 1905, and he then described the decorations on all the supporters of the chamber and two of the passage; these designs included zigzags and a buckler pattern and then two unusual designs—a rayed wheel (or sun?) and, most surprising of all, two feet.[1] These feet are quite clearly represented, and there is no doubt about them. But, alas! the visitor to Le Petit-Mont today will be unable to see more than two of the decorated stones; the Germans in the 1939–45 War used this mound as a strong-point and have incorporated the passage grave into a concrete casemate. The site is now as much a monument of the archaeology of the last war as of the megalith builders. Climb to the top of the mound and look out over the sea to the south of you and over the island-studded gulf to the north of you, to the landscape of Locmariaquer and Carnac to the west, and to the curious passage grave-cum-casemate below. When I last visited this lovely spot I could not but think of Sir Thomas Browne. Here, indeed, is an antiquity which time has antiquated, a minor monument which has been spared; 'these dead bones have . . . quietly rested under the drums and tramplings of three conquests.'

[1] Le Rouzic in *Bulletin de la Société Polymathique du Morbihan*, 1912, and *Corpus des Signes Gravés*, Plates 68–83.

⚜ XI ⚜
More Megaliths

The object of the last few chapters has been to interest visitors to the Carnac area in the main megalithic tombs of the south of the Morbihan. It would have been possible to give an account of how to visit many more megalithic monuments in that classic area; indeed it is impossible not to see far more than have been mentioned here just because they are so common. Map 6 shows the distribution of these tombs in the area; any walk across a sandy pine-clad heath near Carnac is likely to bring you to some interesting site. But of course megalithic monuments in Brittany are not confined by any means to the Carnac area or to the Morbihan: there are well over a thousand megalithic tombs in the five departments that make up Brittany, and the interested traveller should see some of these in Ille-et-Vilaine, Côtes-du-Nord, Finistère and Loire-Atlantique. For these travels he needs the Michelin maps 59, 58 and 67, as well the Vannes-Angers sheet (63) which he has been using for the Carnac area.

Some of the sites most worth visiting are marked on Map 9; in his travels around Brittany in search of more megaliths the traveller should carry with him the green Michelin guide, *Bretagne, Menhirs et Dolmens* by P-R. Giot, and the book on Brittany by the same author in collaboration with J. L. Helgouach and J. Briard. This latter book was first published in English in 1960 in the *Ancient Peoples and Places* series, and is now obtainable in a revised French edition published in 1962 by Arthaud. The small book *Menhirs et Dolmens* consists of a short illustrated text—the illustrations are from the remarkable series of photographs taken by Monsieur Jos le Doaré of Chateaulin. This fine photographer has edited and illustrated many comparable little books in two series *Images de Bretagne* and *Reflets de Bretagne*; they are obtainable in shops all over the Armorican peninsula and make admirable and authoritative guides and souvenirs. Of particular interest to me are *Quiberon-Carnac* by Michel de Galzain, *Ports de Pêche* by André Guilcher, *Pardons de Bretagne* by Florian Le Roy, and *Les Grands Calvaires* and *Croix et Calvaires* by V-H. Debidour.

For those who want to drive around Brittany looking among other things at megaliths the first site to visit outside the Carnac area is Essé between Rennes and Chateaubriant. The local name of this very impressive tomb is La Roche-aux-Fées; it is twelve miles south-east of Rennes, and about two miles from the village of Retiers. It is well signposted, as it should be, being one of the great gallery graves of France; indeed I consider it one of the finest megalithic monuments in the whole of France. Essé is nearly 60 feet long, divided up into an entrance porch and a long parallel-sided gallery with three transverse slabs. No one visiting this site can any longer be in any doubt as to the technical accomplishments of the megalith builders —not that he could have left Carnac with such doubts.

It used to be a standard doctrine among archaeologists that all megalithic tombs—including those completely devoid at the present day of any mound, as is Essé—were originally covered by a mound of earth and stones like the great mound of St-Michel in the Morbihan or West Kennet in Wiltshire or the mound of Barnenez which we shall shortly come to. I am increasingly doubtful of the truth of this classical view and myself doubt whether Essé ever had a mound. If not, it is argued, how could it have been a tomb? But was it a tomb? It has been argued that in Malta megalithic monuments developed from tombs into temples and I think that some of the great French free-standing megalithic monuments like Essé may not have been used primarily as sepulchres. But the reader should be warned that this is a heretical view; the standard view

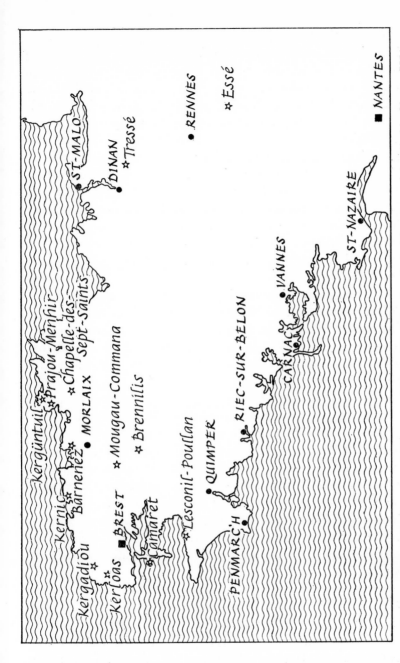

Map 9. *Megalithic sites of special interest outside the Morbihan (marked with a star and described in Chapter XI)*

is that all the French 'dolmens' are tombs and were originally hidden in mounds, long or round.

There is another small version of Essé at Tressé, a village just off the main road from Rennes going north to St-Malo, and some fifteen miles south of St-Malo. (For plans of Essé and Tressé see Fig. 16.) The Tressé monument is locally known as the Maison des Feins and is in the Forêt du Mesnil. This monument is 50 feet long and is divided by a transverse slab into a short and a long chamber; it is partly buried in the ground but also in part covered by an oval mound. One of the most interesting features of this fine *allée couverte* is the carved breasts. There are four pairs sculptured in low relief—two on the inner surface of the east stone of the smaller chamber (or porch) and two on the north side of the cross slab dividing the short and long chambers.

We shall meet sculptured breasts of this kind again in north Brittany. It is an art different from that which we have seen in the passage graves of the Morbihan and is associated with the gallery graves or *allées couvertes* of northern Brittany and the Paris Basin. I have argued elsewhere that these monuments are the tombs (or tombs and temples) of settlers who came from southern Iberia direct by sea to the northern coasts of France, establishing themselves in the north of Brittany, the Channel Islands, and Normandy and penetrating into the Paris Basin and the Champagne area by sailing up the Seine, Oise and Marne. The breasts we find at Tressé and shall see again elsewhere in north Brittany, are like the representations of breasts, faces and necklaces we find in the Paris Basin: part of the iconography of a goddess-figure, the Earth Mother goddess-figure if you like, whose worship began in the most ancient east and the East Mediterranean in the fourth or fifth millennium B.C.

Tressé is the site which was excavated by Miss V. C. C. Collum in 1931. In 1935 she published a book entitled *The Tressé Iron-Age Megalithic Monument*. The average reader will be surprised to find the phrase 'Iron Age' in the title and perhaps understandably be surprised by the subtitle, namely, 'Its quad-

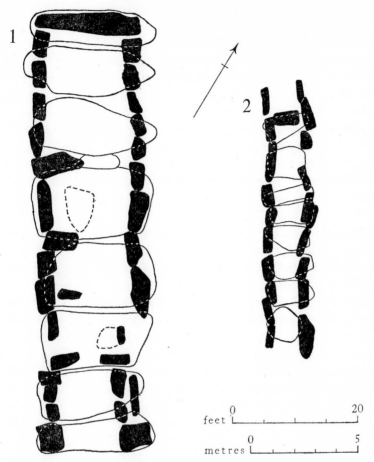

Fig. 16. *Plans of the Gallery Graves at Essé* (1) *and Tressé* (2)

ruple sculptured breasts and their relation to the mother-
goddess cosmic cult'. We have already mentioned Miss
Collum's special ideas on the chronology of megalithic monuments. It has never seemed to me or to most prehistorians that
she made out a case for the late date of this tomb, and there is
no reason to suppose it was built other than somewhere between
2500 and 1500 B.C.

Rennes is conveniently situated between Essé and Tressé. It

is the capital of Brittany and the twelfth largest town in France. It was almost entirely reconstructed on a rectangular grid plan following the great fire of December 1720 which lasted for five days and almost entirely destroyed the small twisting streets of the old city. The new buildings, constructed after the fire, are a little severe and cold, except on a warm day sitting at a café on the quayside of the river Vilaine which, flowing from east to west, cuts the city into two parts. I have spent a lot of time in Rennes, off and on, and have got to like it very much— particularly the remains of the old city around the cathedral. Rennes has two very good restaurants, one of which, the Ti-Koz in the old quarter near the cathedral, is in a house said to be that of Du Guesclin. I particularly remember an extravagant delicious occasion when I dined in the Ti-Koz and ate all the three named specialities of the house listed in the *Guide Michelin*: namely *homard grillé*, *médaillon de ris de veau Ti-Koz*, and *crêpes bretonnes flambées au marasquin*. The other very good restaurant is in the Du Guesclin hotel in the southern half of the city and near the station. The chef there does very good *palourdes farcies* and it is only right that I should confess here and now that this dish is one of the most appreciated in my own personal gastronomy, so that any chef who does hot dishes of oysters, mussels and *palourdes*, particularly when stuffed or with garlic butter, is my man. The chef at the Du Guesclin does many other things extremely well such as soles, and *escalope de veau au vermouth* where the somewhat cloying richness of the Normandy cream sauce is dried away to perfection.

But it is always the discovery of small good restaurants that makes travel in France and elsewhere so rewarding and interesting—not the savouring and evaluation of the starred and reputed establishments. My good friend Dr P-R. Giot whose book on *Brittany* I have already mentioned first introduced me to the Restaurant Au Piré in Rennes (18, Rue Maréchal Joffre), and I have had many very good meals here. It is a medium-sized bourgeois restaurant packed with people at lunch-time, people who appreciate its good value and solid worth.

I have now spent two Christmases in the Morbihan revising this present book, and once, driving back to Paris from Vannes on a cold, misty morning, found we could not get to Rennes in time for lunch. Then began that furious research and comparative study of guide-books and gastronomical guides, which is, admittedly, one of the pleasures of foreign travel, and is now becoming one of the pleasures of British travel armed as we are with the *Good Food Guide* and Egon Ronay's *Guide* and the half-hearted star system in the A.A. Guide. (As if anyone in their right mind wanted to know where the food was better than one might expect it to be from the classification of the hotel: we want to know where eating is taken seriously and food done well.) Our books threw up for us the Hôtel des Forges de Paimpont near Plélan-le-Grand. The *Guide Gastronomique de l'Auto Journal*, which I trust, said we would be very well fed here. The number of cars outside suggested that many other people thought the same. The promise fulfilled the expectation: I vividly remember moving in from the wet and cold outside to the cheerful warmth of a great wood fire and the superb smell of good cooking. We had to walk through the kitchen: it was full of people cooking, eating, drinking, talking. We were given to eat an excellent *terrine* and a quite exceptionally fine *civet de marcassin*. Later on—much later on—we walked into the back yard, and saw the carcase of a deer hanging up in a barn, and a small black wild boar rootling about in a pen.

Turn west from the flesh-pots of Rennes and its neighbourhood to the megaliths of the Côtes-du-Nord. Drive through St-Brieuc and Guingamp and take the road—any road—to Plouaret. From Plouaret it is only five miles to the Chapelle-des-Sept-Saints—a church at the end of a muddy country road and away from everywhere. It most certainly deserves a visit because here we find a megalithic tomb of the general character of Tressé or Essé now built into and forming a functioning part of a Christian church. The church itself was built (or rebuilt?) in 1708 and legend has it that the Sept-Saints are the Seven Sleepers of Ephesus, entombed by the Emperor Decius in A.D. 250. However this may be—and it probably is not—here we have a fine example of a megalithic tomb, belonging to the religious beliefs of the third and second millennia B.C., incorporated in a Christian church and used as part of that church.

This kind of thing is unusual but by no means unknown. Not far from Tressé, on the road from Combourg to Antrain, and near the village of Bazouges-la-Pérouse, is a great menhir 15 feet high surmounted by a cross. Just to the north of Carnac itself is the small megalithic tomb on which a cross has been constructed (Plate 20, top). About twelve miles to the north-northwest of the Chapelle-des-Sept-Saints and between Lannion and Trégastel-Plage is the menhir of St-Duzec (Plate 22) one of the most remarkable examples in Europe of the Christianization of megaliths. This huge menhir is now surmounted by a crucifix and has engraved and painted on it the symbols of the crucifixion. Of course, neither the Chapelle-des-Septs-Saints nor the menhir of St-Duzec means that the megalithic religion survived in real and original and functional form into Christianity (although of course this point of view could be argued), but they must surely mean that the Breton megalithic monuments—tombs, alignments, menhirs—were still a sufficient centre of interest and perhaps private veneration in historical times to make it occasionally necessary and convenient to Christianize them.

From St-Duzec it is easy to visit some more interesting megalithic monuments. One is on the *corniche* road from Trégastel-Plage to Lannion: it is the *allée couverte* of Kergüntuil, which has on its walling-stones several pairs of breasts as well the representation of a necklace; another is on the island of Ile Grande, now joined to the mainland by a causeway, and a third is the site of Prajou-Menhir, discovered only in the last few years, with some remarkable art on the stones of a form not fully understood at the moment.

From Lannion drive west to Morlaix and then north through Plouézoch to Barnenez (Plate 23). Here there were two very fine long mounds, cairns or barrows on the promontory which extends to the north—the Presqu'île de Kernéléhen—from Plouézoch, on the eastern side of the estuary of Morlaix. The

northern of the two long mounds at Barnenez was 100 feet long
by 60 feet broad by 10 feet high and was largely demolished by
a road contractor in 1954, and in so doing it would appear that
he destroyed at least one and probably two passage graves. The
great monument of Barnenez South (Fig. 17), one of the finest
megalithic monuments in north-western Europe, had been
demolished in part by the same road contractor when this
vandalism was halted. The site was then carefully excavated by
Dr Giot and his staff and was shown to be a long mound 270
feet in length from west to east by 75 to 100 feet broad with a
maximum height of 15 to 25 feet, and to contain eleven passage
graves set in a row opening on to the southern side of the
barrow.

Let me repeat—Barnenez South is one of the finest of the
great megalithic monuments of Brittany and is as worthy of a
special pilgrimage as almost any individual site in the Carnac
region. It is particularly intriguing because of the variety of techniques used in the construction of the tombs—corbelled roofs and
capstones obviously being contemporary variants of the same
form—and because it is a site excavated well in modern times,
and thirdly because it is a site discovered only by the chance
operation of a road contractor. If, as most archaeologists believe
at the present day, the prehistoric passage grave set in a round
mound originated in Iberia and spread from there to France,
the British Isles and Scandinavia, then the long mound with a
series of passage graves set side by side (as at Barnenez) is a
development of the French prehistoric megalith builders. We
see the result of this process—the creation of a chambered long
barrow by the accretion of several chambered round barrows
—very well at Barnenez South.

From Morlaix to Brest is an hour's drive of sixty kilometres.
This great French naval port despite its heavy wartime bom-
bardment and the clinical dullness which seems inseparable
from post-war rebuilding, whether it be in Plymouth, Exeter,
Coventry, Abbeville or Brest, still has charm and interest—and
some good restaurants. After all, in Brittany only really bad
restaurants cannot immediately provide a feast of oysters and

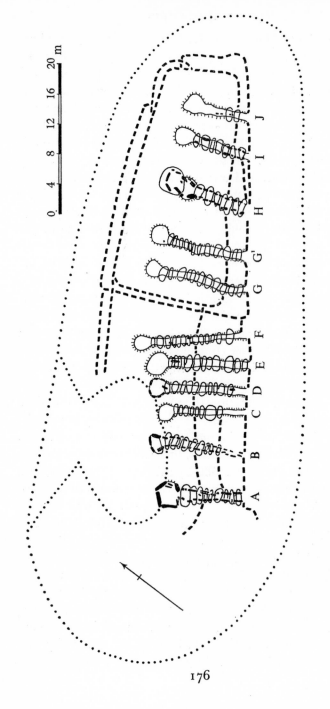

0 4 8 12 16 20 m

176

· · · · outer limit of barrow   – – – revetment walls   ▪▪▪▪▪▪ dry walling

Fig. 17. Plan of the chambered long barrow at Barnenez near Morlaix

shellfish and soles—and perhaps in a country so rich in *fruits de mer* there ought to be, if the law allowed, a register of restaurants not to be visited. Brest itself is full of good small restaurants: find your way to them by following the sailors. For an exceptionally good meal go to the Hôtel des Voyageurs just off the large windswept Place de la Liberté. This is a modern hotel attractively set out; its modern kitchens have a high standard of cooking. Particularly to be recommended are the *soupe de poissons*, the *ficelle brestoise*, and the *queue de langouste amoureuse*—crayfish cooked in five alcohols and liqueurs.

From Brest as a centre it is easy to make expeditions to some of the important and interesting megalithic monuments of northern Finistère. First let us go to the *pays de Léon* north of the great menhir of Kerloas near Plouarzel and the two menhirs at Kergadiou at Plourin-Ploudalamezeau. The Kerloas menhir is 38 feet in height and is dressed; it is the tallest menhir still standing and is second only to the Grand Menhir Brisé at Locmariaquer. One of the menhirs at Kergadiou is still standing and with a height of 34 feet comes next to the Kerloas menhir; the other which measures nearly 30 feet is on the ground. From these menhirs drive through the Léon countryside along the coast or through Le Folgoet to the little town of Plouescat with its remarkable sixteenth-century wooden market. Ask your way to the *anse de Kernic* which is at low tide an immense expanse of sand and dunes: here you will find on the beach the interesting *allée couverte* of Kornig (Roc'hou-Bras). At high tide it virtually disappears beneath the sea and is another reminder of the fact we observed in the Gulf of the Morbihan, particularly at the dramatic site or Er-Lannic, that there have been changes in the relative levels of land and sea in Brittany since the time of the megalith builders.

East of Brest and in the hills between Sizun and Huelgoat are two megaliths that demand a visit; one is the gallery grave of Mougau-Commana and the other the site called Ty-ar-Boudiquet (the house of the fairies) at Brennilis. Mougau-Commana (or Mougau-Bihan, Commana) is a gallery grave 40 feet in length: its special interest lies in the art on its walls which includes the representation of eight long-bladed tanged daggers. The Ty-ar-Boudiquet is a fine monument of the type generally referred to as a V-shaped or undifferentiated passage grave. This is the sort of monument which might be transitional in form between the passage grave with sharply demarcated Passage and Chamber, and the *allée couverte* or gallery grave. Many suggestions have been made as to the origin of the gallery grave form such as we have seen so well represented at Tressé, Essé, Kergüntuil and Mougau-Commana—that the form represents a surface megalithic version of a long rock-cut tomb or that it developed out of the passage grave via such transitional forms as Brennilis. Both explanations are possible and are not mutually exclusive. The long gallery grave form might have arisen in different parts of western Europe in different ways.

The traveller visiting Commana and Brennilis is in a part of Brittany full of interesting things: the Camp d'Artus for example at Huelgoat and the splendid Calvaries of St-Thégonnec and Guimiliau. On a recent visit to this part of Finistère I agreeably coincided with Sunday lunch Chez la Mère Grall at Sizun: it began with a *plateau de fruits de mer* (six oysters, fine crabs, an excellent mayonnaise), a *coquille St-Jacques gratinée*, chicken from the farm with potatoes and salad, and jam pancakes: all for 7 francs.

A very pleasant excursion can be made from Brest by taking the boat across the harbour to Camaret—the journey lasts about forty-five minutes. Less than a mile from the harbour at Camaret are the stone rows of Lagatjar consisting of 140 menhirs set in three lines. This site was restored a few years ago. The main axis is 200 metres in length; two lines run from it at right angles and a third in an oblique direction.

Continuing our tour around Brittany in search of interesting megalithic monuments the traveller should now leave Brest for Quimper via Chateaulin and Douarnenez where he takes the road to Tréboul and on to Poullan-sur-mer. Before getting to Poullan stop at Lesconil to visit the Ty-ar-Chorriquet (the dwarf's house). This site is one of only three that exist in Brittany—all in southern Finistère and of a type known as the *allée couverte arc-bouté*—the other two are Castel-Ruffel near St-Goazec and Goulet-Riec at Riec-sur-Belon. These three gallery graves have no capstones; they are triangular in section and are constructed by having the walling orthostats leaning inwards and touching at the top. In plan however Lesconil in Poullan is a normal gallery grave with a porch and a kerb of stones. From Quimper take the road to Pont-L'Abbé and Penmarc'h, a small town with a fine sixteenth-century church. From here the road leads south-west to the Pointe de Penmarc'h where is the Eckmühl lighthouse, built in 1897 by money provided by the Marquis de Blocqueville in memory of his father, General Davout, Prince d'Eckmühl. From the balcony around the top of the lighthouse one can have a magnificent view of the Penmarc'h peninsula and the coast of southern Finistère from the Ile de Sein to the Iles Glénans. From Penmarc'h a road leads north-west to St-Guenolé—an agreeable sardine fishing and canning port—and beyond to the Musée Préhistorique Finistérien. This is the best archaeological museum in Brittany. It was founded in 1920 by the Groupe finistérien d'Etudes préhistoriques and now is a part of the Faculty of Science of the University of Rennes and under the direction of Dr P-R. Giot. In addition to its well arranged and illuminating collections there have been gathered outside the Museum in its grounds several megalithic monuments including the strange monument of Run-Aour originally at Plomeur. This monument originally had a circular dry-walled chamber, to which two converging passages led, both constructed of megalithic slabs and capstones. The dry-walled chamber has been destroyed but the two passages set up outside the Museum provide a bizarre monument indeed, puzzling to those who do not know its history. A short walk from the museum brings you to the Pointe de la Torche.

From Penmarc'h and Quimper the road leads back to Carnac and Vannes through Concarneau, Quimperlé and Hennebont. The Concarneau and Pont Aven country provides some of the most picturesque of all Brittany and the area has long been frequented by artists. The school of Pont Aven was made famous by Paul Gauguin. The lace coifs of the women of Pont Aven and Quimperlé make market day in either of these towns very fascinating and colourful. Our suggested journey around Brittany in search of more megaliths is now at an end. There could be no nicer place to contemplate its end than at Riec-sur-Belon on the road from Pont Aven to Quimperlé. Here there is one of the three *arc-bouté* gallery graves, here is the home of the famous *belon* oysters, and here too is the famous restaurant Chez Mélanie. It was made especially famous because Curnonsky went to live there during the German occupation of France. Curnonsky's real name was Maurice-Edmond Sailland and he was born in 1862 in Anjou. When he went to Paris as a struggling writer in his twenties there was a vogue for all things Russian. The Czar Alexander III visited the Paris International Exposition in 1889. Sailland thought he might do better with a Russian name and added a -sky to the Latin *cur non?* (why not?). He was awarded the title of 'Prince Elu des Gastronomes' in a contest conducted by one of the great Paris newspapers—a title which it was decided not to use again when he died in 1956 at the age of 84. The elected prince of Gastronomes spent many years at Riec, which is, one would suppose, sufficient commendation for Mélanie's cooking. Mélanie Rouat is herself now dead but her house and fine traditions of cooking are carried on by her daughter Marie. Here you may eat the famous *belons, palourdes farcies, moules 'Mélanie'*, and the *homard 'Mélanie'*—a lobster in a rich cream sauce which Samuel Chamberlain in his wise and valuable *Bouquet de France* calls 'superlative' and many others 'a superb gastronomic experience'. A nice way to end a search for more megaliths—or to begin one if you set out from Carnac to travel round Brittany in the reverse direction from our journey in this chapter.

✣ XII ✣

Conclusion

We have now come to the end of what was our purpose
in this little book, namely to introduce the reader
to some aspects of the prehistory of France through
sites and monuments in two areas, the Dordogne and Brittany,
and to the pleasures of travel in those two areas. It is now time
to wend our way back to England. That journey is very likely
to take in Paris and here there will be a chance to visit two
museums with material of great importance from the Palaeolithic caves and the Breton megaliths.

The first museum is in Paris itself; it is the Musée de L'Homme
and is part of that great foundation the Muséum d'Histoire
Naturelle. The Musée de l'Homme is in the Palais de Chaillot,
the old Trocadéro, and here the visitor will find an extremely
well displayed collection of archaeology and ethnography including much material from the Palaeolithic, and among this
material the fine Venus from Lespugue, and the ibex and man's
head from Angles-sur-L'Anglin.

The second is the Musée des Antiquités Nationales which is
part of the Louvre but situated out at St-Germain-en-Laye.
Twenty minutes in an electric train from the Gare St-Lazare
will bring you to St-Germain-en-Laye, and you emerge from
the railway station on to the Place outside the Château. The
Musée des Antiquités Nationales is housed in the Château, and
like all main French museums is open every day except Tues-
days. Here you will find very rich Palaeolithic collections including some given and arranged by the Abbé Breuil: some of
the finest things from the mobiliary art of Upper Palaeolithic

times are here such as the statuette of a woman from Sireuil, the mammoth from Bruniquel carved in reindeer antler, and some remarkable horses' heads including one on a spear-thrower. Here too you will find the originals of the sculptures from Le Loc de Sers in the Charente which we have already mentioned (p. 180). St-Germain has good collections from the Breton megalithic monuments, and casts of the decorated walling slabs at Gavr'innis, Le Petit-Mont, Les Pierres-Plates and Mané-er-Hroeck. But perhaps its most exciting collections are those that illustrate the end of independent Gaul and the beginnings of the Roman period in France.

It was the Emperor Napoleon III who created a Museum of National Antiquities in St-Germain. He was interested in the brave stand of the Gauls against Julius Caesar and had organized excavations at the native sites of Gergovia and Alésia. It was the material excavated at these sites that did not seem to fit into the scheme of things at the Louvre itself, and so, in 1862, an imperial decree created in the Château de Saint-Germain-en-Laye *'un Musée d'antiquités celtiques et gallo-romaines'*. On the 12 May 1867 Napoleon III formally opened the Museum. In this Museum the French have something which we do not have in Britain, namely a Museum of National Antiquities, although we do, of course, have the Department of British and Medieval Antiquities in the British Museum, and the National Museum of Wales in Cardiff and the Museum of the Antiquities of Scotland in Edinburgh. The St-Germain-en-Laye Musée des Antiquités Nationales is supposed to be under reconstruction as these words are written. It has certainly badly needed reconstruction and modernization for many years; I recollect only too well days of peering in bad light at the dark cases and old-fashioned labels. The Musée de l'Homme, on the other hand, is very well set out, and it, like the Louvre, shows how very good French Museum display can be. This makes it all the sadder that the average French provincial archaeological museum is so bad; we have referred on several occasions to the Vannes Museum where so much material from the early excavations in the Morbihan is housed. This is a ghastly place; ill-lit, with old-

24. Typical Breton food

25. (*a*) Air view of the Château, *place*, Church and River Seine at
St-Germain-en-Laye

25. (*b*) The Gallery Grave of Conflans-Ste-Honorine now in the
moat of the Château of St-Germain

fashioned cases crowded with objects hopelessly displayed and crumbling into decay. When I visited the Vannes Museum last in December 1962 I thought that many of the objects were in a far worse state than they had been before. Vannes and many another comparable museum are quite shocking: they are decayed and dying charnel houses of French antiquarianism. We would not now tolerate such disgraces in England. Vannes should be compared to Devizes—both belong to local archaeological societies. The members of the Société Polymathique du Morbihan who own the Vannes Museum should all be transported by U.N.E.S.C.O. to Devizes and shown how a regional society museum can be run. When last December I tottered out of the Vannes Museum, clutched at the last moment by the *concierge* and reminded of two little trays, one for tips for her, and the other, believe it or not, for the reconstruction and rehabilitation of the Museum, I went across the road to a café, and, reconstructing and rehabilitating myself with a St-Raphael, wrote in my notebook, 'Have I ever been in a worse or more depressing museum in Europe?' On reflection I think I have, and both, alas, are in France; at the other one when I asked for light I was told roundly that I should have brought my candle with me!

Do not suppose that St-Germain is this sort of place. It still has its dark corners and badly arranged cases but there is now a sense of purpose there. I hope I live long enough to see finely displayed collections of prehistoric antiquities both at St-Germain-en-Laye and in Bloomsbury. Before leaving St-Germain you should see the turret room with originals and casts of statue-menhirs, those intriguing carved stones from southern France with their representations of an east Mediterranean goddess figure; and also look down into the moat where some megalithic monuments have been re-built. One is the fine *allée couverte* of Conflans-Ste-Honorine with a well-preserved porthole entrance, moved in 1872 from its original site on the Seine four miles south of Pontoise. Nearby is the *allée couverte* known as Le Trou des Anglais which was discovered at Aubergenville, seven miles east of Mantes on the south bank of the

Map. 10. *Map showing the distribution (shaded areas) of megalithic tombs in western Europe. The black dots indicate specially important sites*

Seine; it was moved the ten miles to St-Germain in 1901 and set up in the moat. These two monuments—Conflans-Ste-Honorine and Aubergenville—are typical of the *allées couvertes* of the Paris Basin, and there are many more of them which can easily be visited from St-Germain or Paris (Plate 25).

It is important not to give the impression that megalithic

monuments in France are confined to Brittany and the Paris Basin. This is far from the truth. They are widespread in France and in other parts of Western Europe as the sketch-map (Map 10) shows. A very pleasant itinerary of France could be devised that wandered around the country from megalith to megalith; it would begin in the Marne and then proceed via the Paris Basin through Normandy to Brittany. There we have already outlined a journey around Brittany; it would end at Carnac with its classic sites. Then on through the Loire-Atlantique to some of the famous sites on the Atlantic coast of Central France like Pornic and Le Bernard (north of La Rochelle) and up the Loire to the great tomb of Saumur. This great gallery grave in the Bagneux suburb of Saumur is one of the finest megalithic tombs in Europe. Its plan is given in Fig. 10 (bottom). This great monument is 61 feet long by 16 feet wide and from 8 feet 6 inches to 9 feet high; it is roofed by four capstones each about 2 feet thick, and the largest of these capstones has been estimated to weigh over 86 tons—its dimensions are 23 feet square by 2 feet 4 inches thick). Saumur, like Essé, makes one believe in the rightness of calling these monuments 'megalithic' (Plate 23).

Our megalithic journey on through France would then go south through Poitiers, Cognac and Angoulême and across through the Dordogne to the *causses* country of the south Central Massif where megalithic tombs abound and where it is thought their construction went on until very late—perhaps as late as 1000 B.C. The south of France is, in popular English imagination, not so rich in megaliths as the north, yet the department of the Aveyron has more megalithic tombs than has the Morbihan, and the statue-menhirs of that department in the Museum at Rodez must be seen. Finally our brief tour could end in the immediate neighbourhood of Arles, not far from Alphonse Daudet's *moulin* where there is a group of tombs including the famous Grotte des Fées, which should not be missed.

But we have digressed a long way from the Château of St-Germain-en-Laye. The Château itself is of considerable interest. It was first built in the twelfth century, then destroyed by the

English in the fourteenth, rebuilt by Charles V, and then destroyed again in the sixteenth century by François I who, keeping the chapel of St-Louis, built the new château which we see at the present day (though enlarged in the seventeenth century and restored in the nineteenth and twentieth centuries). It is of very special interest to us in England because it was here that James II set up his court in exile in 1689, and here he died in 1701. He is buried in the church across the square from the Château, and a plaque on the outside wall of the church records the visit of Queen Victoria to see the tomb in 1855 (Plate 25).

Most visitors to the Musée des Antiquités Nationales will come in the summer and so take a more cheerful view of these bad and poorly arranged collections. If they do not, they can cross the square and sit in the sunshine at one of the café tables and order a carafe of wine. It will not be the Muscadet of Brittany that is brought nor the Monbazillac of the Dordogne, but it will have in it the warmth of the sun and the sweetness of the grape. Lift a glass to the walls of the Château opposite, and to the men who long ago built the great dolmens and alignments at Carnac and painted the bulls at Lascaux.

St-Germain is also a very nice place for lunch when visiting the Musée. I have eaten countless meals in the various café-restaurants on the square; study the bills of fare set outside and make your own choice. I have never found one that was compelling, never met an English or French colleague who has said, 'Of course we must lunch at so-and-so on the Place', but always had good meals, and yet always wondered where I would lunch next time I was at St-Germain. But in the last few years I have been making a practice of walking down the hill and across the Seine to Le Vesinet—it is only just over a mile from the Musée and a very pleasant walk—and lunching Chez Narbonne. Here you will find a very good cuisine—all *à la carte* and therefore more expensive than the *prix fixe* meals up on the Place—but worth it; very good *coquilles St-Jacques*, excellent *quenelles de brochet*, splendid *steack au poivre*. When I next satisfactorily finish a piece of research at St-Germain I shall have no hesitation in celebrating Chez Narbonne, and then after lunch catching the bus back to the Porte de Neuilly and so into Paris and home. But wherever your last meal in France, take back with you the memory of the great painted caves and the great megaliths—archaeological vestiges of a time when France was young, when western Europe was young, and when neither Frank nor Anglo-Saxon had been heard of.

Index

INDEX

HOTELS, RESTAURANTS Etc.